GHOULISH GOODIES

GHOULISH GOODIES

SHARON BOWERS

Storey Publishing

The mission of Storey Publishing is to serve our customers by
publishing practical information that encourages
personal independence in harmony with the environment.

Edited by Margaret Sutherland
Art direction, book design, and photo styling by Alethea Morrison
Text production by Liseann Karandisecky

Photography by © Kevin Kennefick
Food styling by Norma Miller
Illustrations by © Michael Slack

Indexed by Christine R. Lindemer, Boston Road Communications

Printed in China by Regent Publishing Services
10 9 8 7 6 5 4 3 2 1

Library of Congress Cataloging-in-Publication Data

Bowers, Sharon.
  Ghoulish goodies / by Sharon Bowers.
      p. cm.
  Includes index.
  ISBN 978-1-60342-146-1 (pbk. : alk. paper)
  1. Halloween cookery. I. Title.
TX739.2.H34B69 2009
641.5'68—dc22
                              2009007802

Dedication

For Hugh and Pearse, my bright-eyed kitchen helpers,
always happy to lick beaters and taste cupcakes.

Acknowledgments

Many, many thanks to my editor, Margaret Sutherland, unfailingly delightful to work with — and eagle-eyed to boot; to creative director Alethea Morrison, who oversaw the fabulous design; to food stylist Norma Miller and photographer Kevin Kennefick, who made and shot picture-perfect versions of the recipes; to Michael Slack, for the fantastic illustrations and also to the whole dream team at Storey, including Pam Art, Deborah Balmuth, and the ever-encouraging Amy Greeman.

Particular thanks to my agent, Jennifer Griffin, for finding me a good home there, then gently but firmly making sure I got the manuscript finished on time, and to Angela Miller for her humor and constant support. I couldn't have done it without both of them.

Most of all, thanks and love to my husband, David Bowers, for his willingness to undertake and refine the messiest projects, make endless trips to the store to buy yet more sugar and butter and, mostly, just for making life fun.

CONTENTS

INTRODUCTION

On a dark, windy night, dry leaves skitter down the empty pavement with a sound like chattering teeth. A blood-red moon hangs low in the sky and the weak pools of light cast by the streetlamps strain against the velvety blackness. What mischief lurks abroad? Why, it's nothing but a bunch of riotous ghosts, goblins, pirates, witches, and superheroes, laden with swinging bags of candy and heading to a party featuring fresh-baked jack-o'-lantern cookies and spidery cupcakes, not to mention candy apples, homemade caramel corn, and chocolate mice! They've been waiting for this night for weeks on end, and they're not going home until their bags and their bellies are full of goodies.

HALLOWEEN FUN

My kids adore Halloween and it's all my fault — I've encouraged it since they were born. When the autumn afternoons turn dark and cool, I think there's nothing cozier for a family to do together than turn on the kitchen lights, heat the oven, and bake. Throughout October, my boys clamber on the counter and help me make webs on sugar cookies, shape scary monster cupcakes, and stir up pumpkin fudge that's redolent of warm spices. We make wacky chocolate bat cookies and pick the seeds from the pumpkin's innards to make fabulous sweet and spicy toasted pumpkin seeds. They love it; I love it.

Because, of course, adults adore Halloween, too. And why not? Halloween is a good reason to decorate our homes and have a party, which in fact isn't so very far from the original purpose of the holiday. The long-ago festival of Samhain in the Celtic tradition, despite its oft-mentioned association with spirits of the dead, was largely a good excuse to enjoy harvest bounty and visit with neighbors before the cold winter settled in. So America is really following the example of our various ancestors in making

Halloween the third-largest party day in the United States, trailing only New Year's Eve and Superbowl Sunday.

Retailers and journalists continue to marvel at the stunning commercial growth of Halloween in America (we spent nearly $6 billion on it in 2008), but every American child knows from the time he can walk, talk, and chew candy corn that Halloween is *the* event of the year. Thanksgiving and Christmas arrive with the attendant stresses of family gatherings and enormous meals, but Halloween is nothing but joy. It's the first fun holiday that comes along after the kids go back to school, and they throw themselves into it wholeheartedly.

As pumpkins and scarecrows begin to appear on front steps and porches, there's the thrilling anticipation: preparing the costume, wearing it for weeks, even sleeping in it if Mom allows. Then there's the party at school with cupcakes and gift bags of candy corn. And then, on the night itself, there's the unbearable delay of gobbling down a Halloween supper, the dispute over whether you have to wear a coat over your costume or not, then the wild run to the first house to ring the doorbell and shout as shrilly as possible, "Trick or TREAT!"

With luck, you then get to lug your huge bag of candy onward to an after-party with *more* sweets. Add frenzied candy-sorting in front of the TV before bed (doesn't everyone do this? It was the favorite part of the evening in my childhood), the trade-offs with your siblings (one chocolate bar

for three packs of Smarties; the next-door neighbor's homemade caramel corn for a full-size Snickers), and a final piece of candy before sleep — and you have a holiday that's pure childhood bliss.

Parents today remember those joyous and innocent nights and we want to recreate the carefree Halloweens of our youth, with a lot of gently scary fun, delicious food, and the creation of special memories for our own kids. I'm a busy mom and I don't have time to decorate my suburban lawn like the front of a department store. Instead, I like recipes and ideas that are fun for my family and me to make together, and that can help similarly busy parents bring the holiday home again.

Fun, fabulous food helps to set the mood as much as anything. In the same length of time it would take to load up the mini-van and make a trip to a box store to buy a lighted display or a costume, you could make a batch of Wormy Cupcakes or some spooky Witches' Fingers — it's cheaper, and it's much more of a kick for your kids.

POINTERS FOR SUCCESS

Much of the thrill for children comes from the hands-on process of helping to make these goodies, and so these recipes are formulated to leave lots of leeway for little hands to help. Rather than trying to make picture-perfect cookies, I'd rather see my kids have fun making their lopsided versions of each item.

True to that end, everything in this book is good to eat, kid-friendly, *and* manageable for busy cooks — the gross-out factor is at a minimum, there is no complicated styling and sculpting, and deliciousness is at the max. Flavor and visual appeal, ease and child-friendliness *always* trump creepiness, so these dishes will remain spellbindingly addictive for parents and kids, with recipes that families will turn to again and again every Halloween.

With that in mind, here are some thoughts for success.

Try Paste Colorings

If you only have the regular 4-pack (red, blue, yellow, green) of liquid food coloring in your cupboard, go to a specialty baking shop and get paste coloring for the deepest colors. To get really intense colors out of liquid, you have to use so much that you may in fact taste a bitter edge and may also end up with too much liquid in your dough, altering the outcome. Liquid colors are great to add a mild orange glow to a sugar-cookie dough, for example, but if you want to make something really black or deeply orange without materially affecting the quality of the dough, go for paste. A very small amount goes a long way, and the little jars keep indefinitely. Even better, stores such as Wal-Mart and Target are starting to carry Halloween paste colors in their holiday sections.

Go Easy on Foreign Objects

Toothpicks may seem like a good idea when you're trying to stick the marshmallow neck plugs on the sides of your Frankenstein cupcakes, but in the midst of a busy party with lots of noisy kids running around, it's too hard to keep track of who's biting into what — no matter how old your guests are. There's hardly any crafting material you can't replace with an edible object, so use pretzel sticks instead of toothpicks, for example, or royal icing (page 61) as glue, instead of nonfoodstuffs. The tooth you save may be your own!

On Flour and Sugar

All the flour called for in this book is regular old all-purpose flour, unless specifically stated otherwise. Similarly, all the white sugar is regular old granulated sugar. For brown, I personally prefer dark brown to light brown sugar because I feel it packs a bit more flavor, but you can use either. Anywhere you see molasses required, use sulfured or unsulfured, whatever you have in your kitchen — you won't be using it in amounts where the subtle difference will be noticeable. Baking *does* require a bit more care when measuring ingredients than when making, say, a soup, but I structure my recipes to be as foolproof and straightforward as possible. Thus I'll never call for 1¼ teaspoons baking powder if 1 teaspoon will do just fine.

On Butter

I buy salted butter to eat and thus I have salted butter in the refrigerator when it's time to bake. The standard line among professionals is that if you bake with unsalted butter, you have more control over the amount of salt that goes into the recipe. Call me a sodium-junkie, but I've never found using salted butter in a cupcake to be a problem. I use salted butter *and* put in the ½ teaspoon of salt that the recipe calls for, and it's not only fine, it's delicious. My mother avers that unsalted butter is fresher than salted butter, which was originally only salted to improve its "keeping" qualities, but if there ever was a time when different butters by the same manufacturer were of noticeably different freshness levels, well, those days are over. All the recipes here that call for "butter" expect that you'll probably use salted butter and that's just fine. If you do use unsalted butter, taste the batter before baking and ask yourself, "Does this need more salt?" If it does, add some.

On Chocolate and Chocolate Chips

I love high-quality chocolate with high cacao percentages, with distinctive, estate-grown pedigrees and an exquisite mouthfeel. But I have a grade-schooler and a preschooler, so when I open my cupboard doors, I'm far more likely to find a bag of plain old semisweet chocolate chips — which is also the thing I'm far more likely to find when racing into the grocery store. Thus, nearly all of these recipes are formulated for the easiest chocolate to find: chips. If you already have a stash of better chocolate, or if you prefer dark to milk or vice versa, I urge you to use whatever you like best in place of any of the chocolate chips called for here. A regular bag of chocolate chips is 12 ounces, about 2 cups of chips. So you can easily replace any chocolate here with 6 or 12 ounces of whatever you like best. You have my blessing and my envious stare.

On White Chocolate

The experts are always quick to point out that white chocolate isn't really chocolate since it has cocoa butter but no chocolate liquor or any other cocoa product. Okay, so it's not chocolate, but that's what the labels say and that's what we all call it. I use white chocolate chips for melting and decorating, because they have a good balance of sweet and salty that makes them tasty for goodies, but you must be very careful when melting white chocolate. Double boilers are good because you can keep a close eye on the melting chips and whip them off the heat promptly, but I usually melt in the microwave. Start melting the chips on high power for one minute, and then stir very well. Do any additional heating in 10-second bursts, stirring frequently, because what looks like solid chips in the bowl will dissolve into melted chocolate as soon as you stir. Overheating or getting any liquid into the chocolate will cause it to seize into a stiff, ruined mass, and you may have to throw it away and start over, so handle with care. For real ease of use, it's hard for home cooks to beat white "coating" chocolate or white chocolate bark, which doesn't even have cocoa butter. Since it's made primarily of vegetable oil and sugar, it's not the greatest in terms of flavor, but it's easy to melt, won't "seize," and makes for shiny, perfect results.

On Cake Mix

Even though this book is full of varying cake recipes, there's not a one that you can't replace with a cake mix. Whether I call for yellow cake, or white cake, or red velvet cake, or carrot cake, I always offer the homemade version because — although I recognize that there's a seductive ease and speed about cake mix — I don't like cake mix. Mixes may produce a delicate tender crumb and a moist cake, but they taste like all the chemical preservatives and emulsifiers that make them bake up so prettily. Homemade cake is pretty darn easy to make and it's *always* tastier. However, even I am not immune to the ease of opening a box, and I have used cake mixes for last-minute children's birthday parties. So even though I always *try* to make a home-made cake, we should all feel guilt-free, and welcome, to use a cake mix of any flavor for any of the cakes or cupcakes here.

On Purchased Frosting

On the other hand, purchased frosting is a crime, and if you've committed it, I beg you to come back to the right side of culinary law. There is nothing easier than making homemade frosting, and it tastes about . . . oh, I don't know . . . *a million times better*. There's no trick to it. Soften a stick of butter (by which I mean leave it out of the refrigerator for an hour). Beat it in an electric mixer or with a wooden spoon until it's smooth. Stir in one 1-pound box (about 4 cups) of confectioners' sugar, one or two tablespoons of milk, and a little vanilla extract. If you want chocolate, add ½ cup of melted chocolate or ⅓ cup cocoa powder. If you want color, add food coloring as desired. That's it. If it's too thick, add a bit more milk, by the tablespoon, until it's thin enough. If it's too thin, add more

confectioners' sugar. What you want is "a smooth spreading consistency." What's that? That same thing that looks so nice on top of a purchased cake or cupcake — you'll know it when you see it.

The Homemade Decorating Kit

Somewhere in the depths of my kitchen drawers, I'm almost positive that I have a pastry bag with a number of basic decorating tips (professionals call them "tubes") to make nice finishes on cakes. And one of these years I'll find it. Until then, I'll continue to use my homemade version, which is a ziplock bag with a hole cut in one corner. If I want a very thin stream of melted chocolate or liquid icing, I use a toothpick to poke a tiny hole right into the corner seam. If I want a wider stream for thicker icing, I use scissors to cut off the very tip of one of the bag's bottom corners. Always start with a smaller cut since you can widen but can't narrow it. A quart bag works for basic cake decorating, and a gallon size is ideal for larger projects such as the Ghostly Mashed Potatoes (page 132) or the Witches' Knuckles (page 108). Is this going to give you a perfect, super-professional finish? No. Will it give you a result that will make you the envy of all the other moms in the neighborhood? Definitely.

Set Your Own Gross-Out Limit

The limits in this book on what's funny and cool and creepy and yummy, and what's beyond disgusting, are solely mine. Some people *love* kitty litter cake, made with crumbled cake crumbs and softened Tootsie rolls and served up in a new litter box with a newly bought scooper, but I'm just not into it. Nor the bedpan pie, with yellow Jell-O in a newly bought bedpan and Snickers bars set in the gelatin. It sounds funny to write, but I don't want to see it on my table. On the other hand, I

think Puking Pumpkins are nothing short of hilarious and have suggestions for three different ones in the Party Food section on page 140. And I don't mind recommending that you let kids stick their hands in a bowl and feel canned spinach masquerading as "witches' guts." Nonetheless, my overall intent here is for food that's fun but still appetizing and tasty. If you need a kitty litter cake recipe, the Internet is always at your service.

Don't Drive Yourself Nuts

I have two main goals when I throw a party for kids or adults: 1) To have fun, and 2) (maybe this should be 1), Not to drive myself crazy. Everyone has a personal style, but I don't think I'm alone in saying that it's hard to get kids fed and costumed, trick-or-treated, and perhaps on to a party, or even home to host their own. So if I'm *also* trying at the same time to finish a couple of batches of Buried Alive Cupcakes, unmold a Wormy Pie, peel a dozen grapes, make a Graveyard platter of party sandwiches shaped like tombstones *and* finish roasting and saucing a tray of Bat Wings — well, that's what I call making myself crazy. So I urge you to delegate duties and share the load with other parents if you're having a Halloween party. Be willing to accept any offers of help. When someone says, "What can I bring?" the right answer is, "Brownies" or "Cups and napkins," not, "Oh, nothing." After all, it's supposed to be fun for *everyone*. Your kids will remember an afternoon in the kitchen making Glowing Jack-O'-Lantern Cookies with you far longer than they'll remember that you stayed up all night making individual gift bags for every kid who attended.

CANDY
AND GOODIES

When I was a greedy child, I spurned homemade Halloween goodies in favor of amassing packaged stuff in shiny wrappers. It wasn't until I was a greedy adult that I truly realized the value of homemade candy — better flavor, fewer chemical additives, and a lot more fun in the making. Even if your children think they'd rather have a candy bar, they'll join you in the kitchen with joy and gratitude (well, joy) to help dip apples in caramel, shape popcorn balls, or roll plump little chocolate mice in cocoa.

I don't think homemade candy should be a specialty niche, so I shy away from complicated equipment in favor of winging it with what's already on hand (shaping white chocolate ghosts with the back of a spoon, for example). And since I'm a cook who's always had bad luck with traditional fudge recipes, for example, these versions are easy and foolproof. An instant-read thermometer is the one tool that's indispensable for some recipes. For the safest and best results, don't attempt to make Caramel Corn or Pumpkin-Seed Brittle without one.

Not all homemade candy requires a huge effort or a thermometer: there are many easy, tasty, and kid-friendly things you can make that begin with melted chocolate and pretzel

MONSTER EYEBALLS

Use miniature M&Ms (green are fun) to make the irises in these monster eyes and begin with very soft butter, or the ingredients will be difficult to blend. Mound the eyeballs into a bowl for serving, or lay them out on a tray in row after unblinking row.

1½ cups creamy peanut butter
½ cup (1 stick) butter, at room
    temperature
1 (1-pound) package confectioners'
    sugar (about 4 cups)
1 teaspoon vanilla extract

1 (12-ounce) package semisweet
    chocolate chips (2 cups)
2 tablespoons solid vegetable
    shortening
1 (3-ounce) package miniature
    M&Ms

1. Blend the peanut butter with the butter, sugar, and vanilla in a medium bowl. It may be easiest to use your hands (kids love doing this).

2. Line a rimmed baking sheet with wax paper. Roll the peanut butter mixture by teaspoons into small balls and place on the baking sheet. Refrigerate for at least 1 hour to firm up the eyeballs.

3. Put the chocolate chips and shortening in a microwave-safe bowl and melt the chocolate in the microwave: Heat on high for 60 seconds, and then stir well. If it's not quite smooth, heat in two or three 10-second bursts, stirring well after each burst. (Alternatively, you can melt the chocolate, stirring frequently, in a double boiler, over just-simmering water. Avoid overheating, which can cause chocolate to seize up into a stiff mass.)

4. Take the sheet of balls from the refrigerator; use a fork or a toothpick to dip each one most of the way into the chocolate, leaving a round or oval opening of undipped peanut butter on top. (This opening in the chocolate will be the cornea.) Hold each ball over the chocolate to catch the drips, and then return to the wax paper, cornea side up.

5. Place an M&M in the center of the peanut butter cornea to make an iris. Refrigerate for at least 1 hour before serving. Store the eyeballs in the refrigerator or freezer and serve chilled.

Boo-rific Pumpkin-Seed Brittle

Too many recipes for brittle include a big baking soda addition at the end, which makes the hot sugar puff up and become opaque and bubbly. It looks impressive, but it doesn't have the delicate, transparent crispness that brittle-lovers crave. This recipe's tiny amount of baking soda produces the brittle of your dreams. You must have a candy thermometer to make this confection properly.

1 cup granulated sugar
½ cup firmly packed brown sugar
1 cup water
⅓ cup light corn syrup
2 tablespoons butter

1 cup pepitas or 1¼ cups dry-roasted, salted peanuts
½ teaspoon baking soda
1 teaspoon vanilla extract

1. Liberally grease a large rimmed baking sheet.
2. Combine the granulated sugar, brown sugar, water, and corn syrup in a large heavy-bottomed saucepan. Cook over medium heat, stirring constantly, until the sugar has dissolved, and then bring to a full boil.
3. Increase the heat to medium high and continue to boil without stirring until the temperature reaches 260°F on a candy thermometer, 15 to 20 minutes.
4. Remove the pan from the heat to stir in the butter and pepitas with a wooden or other heatproof spoon. Return the pan to the heat and continue to cook, stirring constantly, until the temperature reaches 295°F, about 5 minutes. Remove from the heat and quickly stir in the baking soda and vanilla. Be careful; the vanilla will spatter.
5. Immediately pour the mixture onto the prepared baking sheet. Spread it as thinly as possible with a heatproof spatula, and let stand until completely cool. Break the brittle into serving pieces and store in a ziplock bag, squeezing out the air before sealing, for up to 2 weeks.

Pepitas or Pumpkin Seeds?

Salty pumpkin seeds that you've removed from your own pumpkin and toasted are great for snacking, but skip them here – they're too chewy for the perfectly brittle sugar crust. Pepitas are pumpkin seeds that have been removed from their chewy shells. Their faint green color is perfect in this spooky brittle.

ORANGE POPCORN BALLS

This is a speedy version of popcorn balls, stuck together easily with melted marshmallows, and with the added fillip of orange food coloring for a pumpkinlike appearance. Peanuts add salty flavor and interest, and you can add gummy creatures as well, if you want to ratchet up the horror factor. The dryness of air-popped corn with no added oil is perfect here, but you can use any popcorn you like, including microwave.

10–12 cups popcorn (from ½ cup kernels)

1 cup dry-roasted, salted peanuts

½ cup gummy worms or bugs, optional

3 tablespoons butter, plus more for buttering your hands

1 (10-ounce) package marshmallows red and yellow liquid coloring or orange paste coloring

1. Line a baking sheet with parchment or wax paper. Combine the popcorn with the peanuts and gummy worms, if using, in a large glass, ceramic, or stainless steel bowl (plastic may stain); set aside.

2. Melt the butter and marshmallows in a medium saucepan over medium heat, stirring constantly. Remove the pan from the heat and add 5 drops each of red and yellow liquid coloring or a dab of paste coloring to achieve your desired shade of orange. You can always add more if the marshmallow is not orange enough.

3. Pour the marshmallow cream over the popcorn and mix thoroughly. Working quickly, lightly butter your hands and form balls about 4 inches in diameter. Set the popcorn balls on the baking sheet; allow to cool and firm. Cooled popcorn balls can be wrapped in plastic wrap or wax paper and tied with black or orange ribbon. The balls are best eaten the day they're made.

STICKS AND STONES CARAMEL CORN

Homemade caramel corn outshines the purchased version because it's both tender and crisp, the thin sugar coating giving way to popcorn that melts in your mouth. This colorful version includes candy corn, salted peanuts, and broken pretzel sticks for an addictively sweet and salty taste combination; brown sugar makes a rich, dark caramel. Air-popped popcorn is ideal; the caramel sticks well to it. A digital candy thermometer and a heatproof silicone spatula (or a wooden spoon) for stirring and tossing the hot caramel make this candy super-easy.

1 cup pretzel sticks
8 cups freshly popped popcorn
(from ⅓ cup kernels)
½ cup dry-roasted, salted peanuts
½ cup candy corn

CARAMEL
½ teaspoon baking soda
½ cup (1 stick) butter
2 cups firmly packed brown sugar
2 tablespoons light corn syrup

1. Break the pretzel sticks with your hands into bite-size pieces and put them in a large, heatproof bowl with the popcorn, peanuts, and candy corn.
2. Liberally grease a large rimmed baking sheet or line it with parchment (not wax paper, which sticks). Measure the baking soda and set it in a small dish by your workspace.
3. Combine the butter, sugar, and corn syrup in a large heavy-bottomed saucepan and bring to a boil over medium heat, stirring constantly until the sugar crystals have dissolved. Without stirring, boil until the mixture reaches 300°F on a candy thermometer, 5 to 10 minutes.
4. Immediately remove the pan from the heat, add the premeasured baking soda, and stir briskly. Pour the caramel over the popcorn mixture and mix well, stirring up from the bottom to incorporate the candy corn and peanuts.
5. Quickly pour the caramel corn onto the prepared baking sheet and spread it out to cool. (The process from the time the caramel reaches 300°F through spreading the

mixture on the baking sheet should take about 1 minute.) When the confection has fully cooled, break it into large chunks and serve or store in an airtight container for up to 1 week.

Unpopped Popcorn

Before you add hot caramel to your popcorn, be sure there are not any unpopped kernels left in the bowl. Use your hands to lift the plain popcorn from one container to another, leaving all unpopped kernels at the bottom of the first bowl.

Swamp Creature Toes

Salty, sweet, and nutty, these funny big-toe-like snacks are made extra ghoulish by tossing the almonds with green food coloring to give the end result an eerie glow. Even if you skip the green color, you'll still have funky toes.

½ **cup whole skinless salted almonds**
green liquid coloring
1 **(12-ounce) package semisweet**
chocolate chips (2 cups)
1 **(6-ounce) bag 8-inch pretzel rods**
(about 12)

1. Line 2 baking sheets with parchment or wax paper. Blend the almonds with about 10 drops of coloring in a small stainless steel, ceramic, or glass bowl (plastic might stain). Stir well until all the nuts are coated. Spread the green almonds on a plate to dry.

2. Put the chocolate chips in a microwave-safe bowl and melt the chocolate in the microwave: Heat on high for 60 seconds, and then stir well. If it's not quite smooth, heat in two or three 10-second bursts, stirring well after each burst. (Alternatively, you can melt the chocolate, stirring frequently, in a double boiler, over just-simmering water. Avoid overheating, which can cause chocolate to seize up into a stiff mass.)

3. Break each pretzel rod into 3 pieces. Dip a broken piece about three-quarters of the way into the melted chocolate, leaving a broken end visible. (If it's an end piece of the pretzel, dip the finished end, leaving the broken end showing.)

4. Lay the dipped pretzel on a prepared baking sheet and lay a green almond on the top of the dipped end. If the almond won't stick, dip the underside in a bit more choco-late. When all the toes are decorated, place the baking sheets in the refrigerator or freezer to firm the chocolate. Serve cool.

FUNNY BONES

More fun with pretzels and melted chocolate! Like the pretzel lollipop ghosts, these are a tasty mix of sweet and salty. With the white chocolate coating on them, they are uniformly charming. For the best effect, heap and jumble the little bones in a bowl rather than laying them on a plate. (Although I call for white chips, this is one place where lower grade white "coating" chocolate or bark is so easy to work with that it might be worth the trade-off in taste.)

 1 (12-ounce) package white
    chocolate chips (2 cups)
36 pretzel sticks and rods of various
    sizes
72 mini-marshmallows (about 1 cup)

1. Line a rimmed baking sheet with parchment or wax paper.
2. Place the chips in a double boiler over just-simmering water and melt, stirring frequently. As soon as the chips are just melted (there may even be a few solid ones left), remove the pan from the heat and remove the top section of the double boiler so the chocolate's temperature doesn't keep rising.
3. Stick marshmallows onto both ends of the pretzels, with the marshmallows' flat sides parallel to the pretzel.
4. Dip each pretzel in the chocolate and lift out with a fork, letting the excess drip back in the bowl. Lay the bones on the baking sheet and refrigerate for 30 minutes to harden the chocolate. Store in an airtight container in the refrigerator or at a cool room temperature.

Worse-Than-Its-Bite Chocolate Bark

Chocolate bark is an all-purpose recipe: You can use any kind of chocolate to make it — milk, dark, or white — and you can add just about any ingredient that tastes good with chocolate. The swirling combination of dark and white chocolate, studded with peanuts and raisins, gives this bark an appropriately mysterious Halloween look, but other good spooky additions include any gummy creature (gummy spiders are especially alarming), candy corn, dried cranberries, chow mein noodles, any roasted and salted nut, and orange and black M&Ms. Something salty, such as nuts or chow mein noodles, in each mix is good to relieve the tooth-cracking sweetness! Allow about 1 cup of add-ins to every 3 cups of chocolate chips. (Chocolate chips are what I always have on hand, but this is a forgiving recipe whether you're using your high-end, 60-percent-cacao drops or a big block of no-cocoa-inside chocolate "bark.")

1 (6-ounce) package white chocolate chips (1 cup)
1 (12-ounce) package semisweet chocolate chips (2 cups)

½ cup dry-roasted, salted peanuts
½ cup raisins
½ cup sweetened coconut

1. Line a large rimmed baking sheet with parchment or wax paper. (If using wax paper, grease lightly to prevent sticking.)

2. Place the white chocolate chips in a double boiler over just-simmering water and melt, stirring frequently. As soon as the chips are just melted (there may even be a few solid ones left), remove the pan from the heat and remove the top section of the double boiler so the chocolate's temperature doesn't keep rising.

3. Meanwhile, put the dark chocolate in a microwave-safe bowl and melt it in the microwave: Heat on high for 60 seconds, and then stir well. If it's not quite smooth, heat in two or three 10-second bursts, stirring well after each burst.

4. Stir the peanuts, raisins, and coconut into the dark chocolate and pour it out on the baking sheet, spreading it into a thin layer with a knife or spatula. Working quickly, drizzle the melted white chocolate over the bark. Use a fork to gently swirl the 2 chocolates together, being careful not to overmix. You want the 2 colors to remain distinct.

5. Refrigerate the bark for 20 minutes, and then break into serving pieces. Chocolate bark can be kept in an airtight container for up to 2 weeks.

Don't Have a Double Boiler?

You do, of course. A double boiler is as simple as a saucepan and metal or heatproof glass bowl that's slightly larger than the pan. Put an inch of water in the saucepan, put the bowl with the chocolate in it on top, and bring the water to a boil. Only steam should touch the bottom of the bowl, not the actual boiling water. You can test this by filling the saucepan, setting the bowl on top, and then lifting it. If the bowl is wet, pour out some water, dry the bottom, and test again.

(Don't get water in the bowl, which will make the chocolate stiffen up.)

A metal bowl conducts the heat more quickly, but for chocolate a heatproof glass bowl can be better because the chocolate will melt more slowly and evenly. Slow and steady wins the race with melting chips — keep stirring until there are a few lumps remaining, then remove the bowl from the water and keep stirring until smooth.

White-as-a-Sheet Ghost Lollipops

Kids are crazy about these super-simple lollipops, free-formed from melted white chocolate. You can use paper lollipop sticks if you have them, but the ghosts are even easier and tastier when you use salted pretzel sticks. White chocolate can be a little tricky to work with; pay close attention while melting it because overheating will cause it to seize up. If it does form a stiff mass, butter your fingers and shape it into ghosts anyway — they won't be glossy but they'll taste good. White "coating" chocolate will melt more smoothly, but chips taste better here: your call.

> 1 (12-ounce) package white
> chocolate chips (2 cups)
> 12 (3-inch) pretzel sticks
> 24 miniature chocolate chips

1. Line 2 baking sheets with parchment or wax paper.

2. Place the white chocolate chips in a double boiler over just-simmering water and melt, stirring frequently. As soon as the chips are just melted (there may even be a few solid ones left), remove the pan from the heat and remove the top section of the double boiler so the chocolate's temperature doesn't keep rising.

3. Drop a generous tablespoon of melted chocolate on the parchment. Use the back of your spoon to shape the ghost from the melted chocolate: Drag the back of the spoon slightly downward and sideways to form a curved tail; push the chocolate up and over with the back of the spoon to shape a head and two little hands.

4. Push a pretzel stick into the tail, burying the pretzel about 1½ inches in and spooning a bit more chocolate over to cover it. (You'll have a relatively short 1½-inch handle to hold, but these ghosts don't last long!) Press 2 miniature chocolate chips into the head for eyes.

continued from previous page

5. Continue working until you've used all the melted chocolate, making 6 ghosts on each baking sheet. If the chocolate firms up before you've finished, set it back over the hot water in the double boiler and stir again, being careful not to overheat it.

6. Place the baking sheets in the refrigerator for about 15 minutes, until the ghosts are firm, and serve cool.

Lollipop, Lollipop

Inexpensive Halloween lollipop molds are readily available in September and October, and will give your little ghosties a polished, professional look. You may want to venture out to your nearest baking-supply store and pick up a mold before you melt a single morsel of white chocolate.

Rocky Road-to-Perdition Fudge

Traditional fudge is a demanding confection. It has to be cooked according to highly specific instructions, and then vigorously beaten "until it loses its gloss" — or not. I've had pans of fudge set up to rock-hardness *in* the saucepan (nearly impossible to remove), and have had others remain in a sluggish, caramel-like state no matter how long I whipped it with a wooden spoon. So I've turned at this stage of my life to what I think of as "busy-mom fudge." This kind of fudge, which might also be called Frightfully Foolproof, never fails to set up beautifully, thanks to the additions of chocolate chips and marshmallow cream. It's pretty forgiving about how long you cook it and totally open to embellishments such as nuts and dried cherries. Best of all, nobody seems able to tell the difference between this and the labor-intensive kind.

1 cup mini-marshmallows
3 cups sugar
1 (7-ounce) jar marshmallow cream
½ cup evaporated milk
½ cup (1 stick) butter

1 (12-ounce) package semisweet chocolate chips (2 cups)
½ cup chopped roasted walnuts or almonds

1. Grease a 9-inch square baking pan. Sprinkle the marshmallows evenly over the bottom of the pan and put the pan in the freezer.

2. Combine the sugar, marshmallow cream, milk, and butter in a heavy-bottomed saucepan over medium heat. Stir gently with a wooden spoon until the sugar has dissolved; stop stirring and bring the mixture to a boil. Boil for 5 full minutes without stirring. If the mixture threatens to boil over, turn the heat down slightly.

3. Remove the pan from the heat and stir in the chocolate chips and nuts, mixing until the chocolate melts. Pour the chocolate mixture evenly over the marshmallows in the prepared pan, smoothing the surface with a buttered spatula, and refrigerate until hardened, several hours. Cut into 36 or 48 pieces. Store, tightly covered, in the refrigerator.

PUMPKIN SPICE VANILLA FUDGE

Another foolproof fudge, this version has intriguing fall flavors of pumpkin, warm spices, and toasted nuts, producing a beautiful, not-too-sweet candy. The finished fudge is pale orange from the pumpkin, and freckled with spices and sweet crunchy pecans. You can also use walnuts or almonds, or even cashews, to great effect. If you like, you can replace all the spices with 2 teaspoons of pumpkin pie spice (page 87).

- 3 cups sugar
- ½ cup (1 stick) butter
- ½ cup evaporated milk
- ¼ cup canned pumpkin purée (not pumpkin pie filling)
- 1 (7-ounce) jar marshmallow cream
- 1 teaspoon ground cinnamon
- ½ teaspoon ground ginger
- ¼ teaspoon ground allspice
- ¼ teaspoon ground nutmeg
- ⅛ teaspoon ground cloves
- 1 (12-ounce) package white chocolate chips (2 cups)
- 1 cup toasted pecans
- 1 teaspoon vanilla extract

1. Grease a 9-inch square baking pan.
2. Combine the sugar, butter, milk, pumpkin, marshmallow cream, cinnamon, ginger, allspice, nutmeg, and cloves in a heavy-bottomed saucepan over medium heat. Stir constantly with a wooden spoon until the sugar has dissolved; stop stirring and bring the mixture to a boil. Boil for 5 full minutes without stirring. If the mixture threatens to boil over, turn the heat down slightly.
3. Remove the pan from the heat and blend in the white chocolate chips, pecans, and vanilla, stirring until the chips are completely melted. Pour the fudge into the prepared pan and refrigerate until firm, several hours. Cut into 36 or 48 pieces. Store, tightly covered, in the refrigerator.

CARAMEL APPLES

I don't think about caramel apples for the entire year until the leaves start to fall and the farmers' markets are bursting with crisp autumn apples, and then I crave that intoxicating bite of sweet, chewy caramel and crisp, tart, juicy apple. Just one will do, but it has to be perfect — this is that perfect recipe. (If you don't have or can't find wooden popsicle sticks, use forks — they make a great substitute, and since you'll be eating these pronto, they'll be returned to your flatware service almost immediately!)

6 small, tart, juicy apples (I like Honeycrisp or Gala, but use any crisp apple you like)
6 wooden sticks
1 cup sugar

½ cup (1 stick) butter
1 cup light corn syrup
1 cup heavy cream
1 teaspoon vanilla extract

1. Line a baking sheet with parchment or wax paper. (If using wax paper, butter lightly to prevent sticking.) Wash the apples well in hot water, polishing them with a dry cloth, and push the sticks down into the center of the stem end. Set the apples on the prepared baking sheet and refrigerate while you make the caramel.

2. Butter the sides of a large, heavy-bottomed saucepan and in it combine the sugar, butter, corn syrup, and ½ cup of the cream. Bring to a boil over medium-high heat and cook, stirring frequently, until the mixture reaches 255°F (hard ball) on a candy thermometer, about 30 minutes.

continued from previous page

3. Remove the pan from the heat and stir in the remaining ½ cup of cream and the vanilla. Be careful; the mixture will spatter. Stir well to combine. Return the pan to the heat and continue to cook until the mixture returns to the hard-ball stage, 255°F.

4. Using a potholder, carefully tip the saucepan by the handle to pool the caramel on one side and twirl each apple in the hot caramel. Set them back on the lined baking sheet and allow to harden in the refrigerator.

Quick and Easy Caramel Apples

You can, of course, make good caramel apples with packaged caramels, and if you microwave them it's even faster. Unwrap each caramel from a 14-ounce bag and place them in a microwave-safe bowl with 2 tablespoons of milk. Heat on high for 2 minutes, and then stir briskly. Microwave in 30-second bursts until completely melted and smooth, stirring after each burst. Dip 6 apples in the hot caramel and place on a baking sheet lined with buttered parchment or wax paper. Chill until firm.

Rice Krispie Jack-O'-Lanterns

"Plain Rice Krispie bars are good enough for me and may I never want better!" was my cry until a friend told me how to make little orange jack-o'-lanterns out of the usual back-of-the-box recipe, and my heart melted like a marshmallow. It's gilding the lily to make a small second batch so you can shape green stems for the top of each pumpkin, but stems are the final touch that puts these crowd-pleasers over the top. Kids go wild for helping to make them — what could be more fun than molding something so yummy? The jack-o'-lanterns are so doggone cute you won't want to eat them. But you will.

PUMPKINS
- 1 (10-ounce) bag marshmallows
- 3 tablespoons butter plus more for your hands
  red and yellow liquid coloring or orange paste coloring
- 6 cups crispy rice cereal, such as Rice Krispies (you'll use most of one 12-ounce box for the complete recipe, including stems)

STEMS
- 2 cups marshmallows
- 1½ tablespoons butter
  green liquid or paste coloring
- 2 cups crispy rice cereal, such as Rice Krispies
- ½ cup semisweet chocolate chips

1. Line a baking sheet with wax paper.

2. To make the pumpkins, melt the marshmallows and butter together in a large saucepan over low heat, stirring constantly. Remove from the heat and mix in 6 drops of red and 3 drops of yellow coloring or a dab of orange paste; add more coloring if you want a deeper orange shade.

3. Pour in the cereal and stir quickly to combine. Butter your hands and scoop up about ½ cup of the mixture (it cools quickly; you should be able to handle it) and form into a rounded pumpkin shape with a dent in the top for the stem. Press lightly so the pumpkins don't become too dense. Place on the baking sheet. You should be able to make 12 pumpkins.

continued from previous page

4. To make the second batch for the stems, melt the marshmallows and butter together in a smaller saucepan over low heat, stirring constantly. Remove from the heat and mix in 6 to 8 drops of green liquid coloring or a dab of paste to get a bright shade.

5. Pour in the cereal and stir quickly to combine. Butter your hands and shape a long tapered stem for each pumpkin (the stem should be about as long as the pumpkin is high), pressing them into the pumpkin tops while the stems are still slightly warm. Give the stems an elegant curve.

6. Make the faces. Put the chocolate chips in a microwave-safe bowl, and melt the chocolate in the microwave: Heat on high for 60 seconds, and then stir well. If it's not quite smooth, heat in two or three 10-second bursts, stirring well after each burst. Let the chocolate cool slightly and pour it into a small ziplock bag. Cut off a very tiny bit of one corner of the bag to allow a slender line of chocolate to emerge. Pipe grinning chocolate faces on your jack-o'-lanterns.

7. Cool completely before gobbling down at once or storing in an airtight container for 3 to 4 days.

Make Mine Paste!

Liquid food coloring that comes in the little 4-pack of red, blue, green, and yellow is a standard pantry item in many households. But if you want more intense shades of color — such as orange or black — that don't affect the quality of the food, paste is the professional secret. Once available only in professional bakeshops or by mail order, paste colorings are increasingly available in well-stocked grocery stores and even, around the holidays, in specialty baking sections in big-box stores. When you first try paste color, you may be surprised at the intensity of the shades you can achieve with just a dab. Be sure to start gingerly, with tiny amounts, and build up to your desired shade.

CHOCOLATE MICE

These white and brown chocolate mice are a bit like truffles but with adorable candy additions for ears and tails.

1 (6-ounce) package semisweet chocolate chips (1 cup)
¼ cup sour cream
12 chocolate wafer cookies, crushed into fine crumbs
½ cup unsweetened cocoa

½ cup confectioners' sugar
butter for greasing your hands
24 red hots, mini chocolate chips, or mini M&Ms
24 almond slices
red or black string licorice

1. Line a baking sheet with parchment or wax paper.
2. Put the chocolate chips in a microwave-safe bowl, and melt the chocolate in the microwave: Heat on high for 60 seconds, and then stir well. If it's not quite smooth, continue to heat in two or three 10-second bursts, stirring well after each burst. (Alternatively, you can melt the chocolate, stirring frequently, in a double boiler, over just-simmering water. Avoid overheating, which can cause chocolate to seize up into a stiff mass.)
3. Stir in the sour cream and cookie crumbs, and refrigerate the mixture until firm, no more than 15 to 20 minutes. Do not leave the chocolate in the refrigerator indefinitely; it will become too hard to work with.
4. Place the cocoa on one plate and the sugar on another plate.
5. Butter your hands and roll the chocolate mixture into 12 ovals, tapered to a point at one end and rounded at the other. Lay the chocolate shapes on the prepared baking sheet.
6. Roll 6 of the mice in cocoa and 6 in sugar. Stick 2 red hots just above the tapered end for eyes, and place 2 almond slices behind them at pert angles for ears. Poke a 2- to 3-inch length of licorice into the rounded end for a tail. Chill the mice in the refrigerator to keep them firm until you serve them. Store in an airtight container in the refrigerator for up to 1 week.

PUMPKINS IN THE FIELD

Butterscotch-flavored haystacks make a whimsical base for candy pumpkins. You can set a pumpkin in the middle of each haystack, as if it's sitting in a nest, or let the pumpkin sit in front, as if it's nestled against the foot of the haystack. Although the instructions have you dropping the stacks on parchment, if you're transporting these to a party, it is easier to drop each stack into a paper muffin cup, and then press a candy pumpkin on top.

1 (6-ounce) bag butterscotch morsels (1 cup)
2 cups chow mein noodles
1 cup dry-roasted, salted peanuts

24 candy pumpkins, such as Brach's Mellowcreme Pumpkins (you'll use about half of one 11-ounce bag)

1. Line 2 baking sheets with wax paper or parchment.
2. Put the butterscotch morsels in a microwave-safe bowl, and melt them in the microwave: Heat on high for 60 seconds, and then stir well. If the butterscotch is not quite smooth, continue to heat in two or three 10-second bursts, stirring well after each burst. (Alternatively, you can melt the butterscotch, stirring frequently, in a double boiler, over just-simmering water. Avoid overheating, which can cause the chips to seize up into a stiff mass.)
3. Stir the chow mein noodles and peanuts into the melted butterscotch and drop the mixture by heaping tablespoons onto the prepared baking sheets. While the haystacks are still warm, place a pumpkin on the top or pressed against the side of each treat. Refrigerate to cool and harden, about 20 minutes, and serve chilled. Store in an airtight container in the refrigerator for up to 1 week.

CHOCOLATE SPIDER CLUSTERS

Similar to the butterscotch haystack bases for Pumpkins in the Field but with a more arachnid vibe, these spidery clusters get their creepy appeal from gleaming red candy eyes. If you have time before the chocolate sets up, pull a few chow mein noodle "legs" upward from each cluster to wave around.

1 (6-ounce) package semisweet chocolate chips (1 cup)
2 cups chow mein noodles
¼ cup red hots or red mini M&Ms

1. Line 2 baking sheets with wax paper or parchment.
2. Put the chocolate chips in a microwave-safe bowl, and melt the chocolate in the microwave: Heat on high for 60 seconds, and then stir well. If it's not quite smooth, continue to heat in two or three 10-second bursts, stirring well after each burst. (Alternatively, you can melt the chocolate, stirring frequently, in a double boiler, over just-simmering water. Avoid overheating, which can cause chocolate to seize up into a stiff mass.)
3. Stir the chow mein noodles into the melted chocolate and drop the mixture by table-spoons onto the prepared baking sheets. Press 2 red candies onto one edge of each cluster to make eyes and lift a few chow mein legs up to give a spidery impression. Refrigerate to cool and harden, about 20 minutes, and serve chilled. Store in an air-tight container in the refrigerator for up to 1 week.

WRAPPED CARAMELS

Purchased caramels can be fine — something sugary to eat when you need a pick-me-up — or they can have a sort of chemical undertaste that ruins all the fun. Homemade caramels are something else entirely: rich, brown, buttery, with that true almost-burnt sugar tang in the back of your throat that leaves caramel lovers unwrapping *just* one more. For the cook, wrapping these little goodies is half the fun. Use orange plastic wrap if you find it in your grocery store around Halloween, regular plastic wrap, parchment, wax paper, or foil. The wrapping is necessary to keep the caramels from running together, so don't skip it. For best results, make these on a cool, dry day.

½ cup (1 stick) butter (plus more for greasing pans)
1 cup sugar
1 cup heavy cream

¾ cup light corn syrup
⅛ teaspoon salt
1 teaspoon vanilla extract

1. Heavily butter a glass or metal 8-inch square baking pan and line with foil. Butter the foil too and set the pan aside.

2. Butter the sides of a large, heavy-bottomed saucepan and in it combine the butter, sugar, ½ cup of the cream, corn syrup, and salt. Stir constantly over medium-high heat until the sugar and butter have melted and combined. Dip a clean pastry brush in hot water and use it to wipe down the inside of the saucepan to make sure there are no stray undissolved crystals of sugar clinging to the sides (one crystal can make the whole mass seize up).

3. Continue stirring while bringing the mixture to a gentle boil; cook, stirring gently and frequently, until the temperature reaches 242°F (firm ball) on a candy thermometer, about 30 minutes.

4. Remove the pan from the heat and stir in the remaining ½ cup of cream and the vanilla with a wooden spoon. Be careful; the mixture will spatter. Return to the heat and continue to cook until the mixture reaches 246°F on a candy thermometer, 15 to 20 minutes more.

5. Pour the caramel into the prepared pan, being careful not to scrape the bottom of the saucepan (that caramel at the very bottom will be hotter and will have a different texture, which will be evident when you cut the caramels). Allow to cool completely at room temperature, 3 to 4 hours. Score the surface of the caramel into squares with a sharp knife, and then cover the pan with plastic wrap and chill overnight in the refrigerator.

6. The next day, lift the foil from the pan, peel it off the caramel, and place the square of caramel on a cutting board. Oil a large, sharp knife and cut the caramel into squares, using a sawing motion. Wrap each one individually in parchment, foil, wax paper, or plastic wrap.

Gilding the Lily

To make these caramels into a gourmet treat for grown-ups, sprinkle the top of each one with a few grains of sea salt or fleur de sel just before wrapping.

COLD-AS-A-WITCH'S-HAT CONES

These silly little confections are gone almost as soon as you make them, but they're an entertaining dessert for the whole family; they make everyone smile. They also make a fun party snack and activity, with all the children — and adults, of course — decorating their own funny, witchy faces before flipping them over and devouring them. There are no set quantities: you can make as many or as few witch cones as you like depending on how many eager little hands are waiting! If you can't find licorice strings, look for Twizzlers Pull-N-Peel and separate the strings.

> **pistachio ice cream, or green mint chocolate chip**
> **candy corn**
> **chocolate chips**
> **red or black licorice whips**
> **pointy sugar cones**

1. Line a baking sheet with wax paper or parchment and place rounded scoops of ice cream on it. Freeze until firm, at least one hour.

2. Allow each child (or adult) to decorate a scoop of ice cream with licorice strings on top for hair, candy corn for a nose, chocolate chips for eyes, and red licorice for a mouth. Press a sugar cone on top for a hat, and grin at how cute it is. Flip over and eat immediately!

CHAPTER 2

COOKIES

We use the term "cookie cutter" to mean that something is devoid of character, style, and originality. I don't want anything that's "cookie cutter" in my life — in fact, I don't even want cookie cutter cookies! It was a big breakthrough for me to realize that I didn't need specially shaped cutters to make special cookies. With the tip of a sharp paring knife and a bit of imagination, you, too, can make a huge variety of cookies that all look a bit different: stylish, original, and fun.

The most surprising thing is how good your homemade efforts look. You might have a few lopsided creations, but most of them will be easily recognizable — and very impressive. Make a pumpkin patch of jack-o'-lanterns with glowing candy eyes or a graveyard full of shortbread tombstones, even a cave's worth of rich chocolate cookie bats, all without specialized equipment and with nothing more than a sure and steady hand. Get ready to make the cut!

GINGERBREAD JACK-O'-LANTERNS

This pumpkin patch of jack-o'-lanterns is full-flavored and rich with warm spices. Kids love any cookie with icing, but these are also perfect for grown-ups to enjoy with a cup of tea. Make some short and wide, others tall and thin. Don't go for realism — make your pumpkins more of a caricature, with a big indentation to indicate top and bottom, and a wider, thicker stem than you think would necessarily be on a real pumpkin. When the cookies bake, they'll look just right.

½ cup (1 stick) butter, at room temperature
½ cup granulated sugar
½ cup firmly packed brown sugar
1 egg
1 tablespoon molasses
2¼ cups all-purpose flour
½ teaspoon baking soda
 pinch of salt
1 teaspoon ground cinnamon

½ teaspoon ground ginger
¼ teaspoon grated nutmeg
¼ teaspoon ground cloves
1 recipe Royal Icing (page 61)
 red, yellow, and green liquid food coloring or orange and green paste coloring
 chocolate chips or candy corn to decorate

1. Beat together the butter, granulated sugar, brown sugar, and egg in a large bowl until fluffy. Stir in the molasses.
2. Sift the flour, baking soda, salt, cinnamon, ginger, nutmeg, and cloves into a small bowl, and then blend into the butter mixture. Wrap the dough in plastic wrap and chill for 3 to 4 hours.
3. When ready to bake, preheat the oven to 325°F and lightly grease 2 baking sheets.
4. This is a tender dough, so work quickly to roll it to a thickness of about ¼ inch on a lightly floured surface (if it's too soft to handle, put the dough back in the refrigerator for 20 to 30 minutes). Use a sharp paring knife to cut out pumpkin shapes freehand (you can also use a pumpkin-shaped cutter, of course). If cutting freehand, don't make the stems too thin — they will break off after baking.

5. Carefully lift the pumpkins with a spatula and transfer them to the prepared baking sheets. Bake for about 10 minutes, being careful not to overbake — the cookies should be a pale gold, not brown. Cool completely on wire racks before decorating.

6. To decorate the pumpkins, set aside ⅓ cup of the royal icing and color it green with liquid or paste coloring. Color the remaining icing orange by blending in 5 drops of red and 6 drops of yellow liquid coloring or a dab of orange paste, adding more color to get the shade you like.

7. Spread orange frosting over the pumpkins, avoiding the stems. Allow to set before spreading green frosting on the stems.

8. Press on chocolate chips or candy corn to make a face on each pumpkin, or pipe a face on with melted chocolate using the following method: Put ½ cup of chocolate chips in a microwave-safe bowl and heat on high in the microwave in 10-second bursts, stirring well after each burst. Spoon the melted chocolate into a ziplock bag. Seal the bag, pressing out any air. Use a toothpick to make a very tiny hole in one corner of the bag to release a thin stream of chocolate. Pipe eyes and noses and jagged grins as desired. Allow the chocolate to set before stacking the cookies. Store in an airtight container for up to 1 week.

Monster Toes

Similar to the delicately creepy Ladies' Fingers (page 62), these are bigger, stumpier monsters, more colorful and kid-friendly since they're made from chunky peanut-butter cookie dough with a big, hulking toenail made out of a peanut M&M. While Ladies' Fingers have a thrilling "Eeuww" factor, these elicit more of a "Yum!"

1 cup (2 sticks) butter, at room temperature	2 eggs
1 cup peanut butter, crunchy or smooth	1 teaspoon vanilla extract
1 cup granulated sugar, plus more for rolling	2¼ cups all-purpose flour
1 cup firmly packed brown sugar	1 teaspoon baking powder
	½ teaspoon salt
	peanut M&Ms (you'll need about half of an 11-ounce bag)

1. Preheat the oven to 350°F.

2. Cream the butter, peanut butter, granulated sugar, and brown sugar in a large bowl until fluffy. Beat in the eggs until combined and then add the vanilla.

3. Blend in the flour, baking powder, and salt. Roll the dough into toe-shaped ovals about 1½ inches long, and then slightly elongate and flatten each into a rough toe shape. Roll each toe in sugar and place on baking sheets, leaving at least 1 inch between cookies.

4. Press an M&M near the end of each cookie to make a toenail, and then lightly press and crease the middle of each cookie with a fork to make a knuckle about halfway up. Bake for 8 to 10 minutes, until you just begin to detect a finished cookie smell in the kitchen. Do not brown the cookies. Transfer to wire racks to cool; the cookies will firm up further as they sit. Store in an airtight container for up to 1 week.

GLOWING JACK-O'-LANTERN COOKIES

Simple butter cookies with a hint of lemon are colored orange and cut like jack-o'-lanterns. Use the tip of a knife to cut the shapes freehand and your jack-o'-lanterns will have lots of personality. They take on added luster — literally! — when you crush and melt hard candies in the spaces for the eyes, nose, and grinning mouth. The stained glass effect is beautiful and surprisingly effective given the simplicity of the process. Use lemon drops for a yellow gleam and to ramp up the flavor, or, if you prefer, try butterscotch candies for an orange glow. Let your kids work off some energy crushing the candies while you prepare the dough.

⅓ **cup hard candies**
½ **cup (1 stick) butter, at room temperature**
1 **cup sugar**
1 **egg**
1 **teaspoon lemon zest, optional**

1 **teaspoon lemon juice**
red and yellow liquid coloring or orange paste coloring
2 **cups all-purpose flour**
1 **teaspoon baking powder**
½ **teaspoon salt**

1. Preheat the oven to 350°F. Line 2 baking sheets with parchment, foil, or a Silpat mat (not wax paper, which will stick).

2. Unwrap the candies if wrapped, put them in a heavy ziplock bag, and crush them into powder with the flat side of a meat tenderizer or the bottom of a saucepan.

3. Beat the butter and sugar in a large mixing bowl until creamy, and then blend in the egg, lemon zest, if using, lemon juice, and food coloring. Begin with 6 drops of red and 5 drops of yellow liquid coloring or a dab of orange paste; add more to achieve your desired shade. Stir well until fully combined.

4. Add the flour, baking powder, and salt to the bowl, and mix well.

5. Roll half of the dough out on a lightly floured surface and cut out 8 big jack-o'-lantern shapes with a cookie cutter, or freehand with the tip of a paring knife. Make short, fat pumpkins about 4 inches wide by 3 inches high, or make tall, thin pumpkins about

continued from previous page

4 inches tall and 2 to 3 inches wide. You want some variety here! Use the knife to cut out big eyes, nose, and mouth in each (don't do a lot of teeth — they tend to break off). Keep in mind that you want the eyes, nose, and mouth to be wide enough to hold the melted candy. Carefully lift the pumpkins with a spatula and transfer them to the prepared baking sheets. Use the tip of the paring knife to push back the eye, nose, and mouth openings to make them as wide as possible without losing the bridges of dough between the features. Repeat with the remaining dough half.

6. With the tip of a small spoon, sprinkle candy powder generously into the eyes, nose, and mouth openings, directly onto the parchment. Try to keep the candy off the surface of the cookies.

7. Bake for 8 to 10 minutes, watching carefully. Remove as soon as the candy has melted; don't let the surface of the cookies brown. They should be just set and very pale.

8. Cool the cookies on the baking sheets, or carefully lift the parchment off the sheets and transfer the whole sheet to cooling racks (only if the racks are big enough to hold the sheet). When the cookies are completely cool, carefully peel off the parchment.

SPIDERWEB SUGAR COOKIES

The simple technique of dragging a toothpick through chocolate on a white-frosted surface is fast and easy, but it results in a deliciously professional design that delights kids when they realize that they can do it themselves.

½ cup (1 stick) butter, at room temperature
1 cup sugar
1 egg
1 teaspoon vanilla extract
2 cups all-purpose flour

1 teaspoon baking powder
½ teaspoon salt
1 (6-ounce) package semisweet chocolate chips (1 cup)
1 recipe Royal Icing (page 61)

1. Beat the butter and sugar in a large mixing bowl until creamy. Add the egg and beat until fluffy. Blend in the vanilla. Sift in the flour, baking powder, and salt, mixing just until combined. Divide the dough in half, wrap each piece in plastic wrap, and chill for 60 minutes.

2. Preheat the oven to 350°F and grease 2 baking sheets.

3. On a floured surface, roll out one of the dough halves to a thickness of about ⅓ inch. Cut into circles using a 3-inch round cookie cutter or the top of a drinking glass. Gather and reroll the scraps. Repeat with the remaining dough half.

4. Carefully lift the cookies with a spatula and transfer them to the prepared baking sheets. Bake for about 8 minutes, until light golden. Do not overbake.

5. Put the chocolate chips in a microwave-safe bowl, and melt the chocolate in the microwave: Heat on high for 60 seconds, and then stir well. If it's not quite smooth, continue to heat in two or three 10-second bursts, stirring well after each burst. (Alternatively, you can melt the chocolate, stirring frequently, in a double boiler, over just-simmering water. Avoid overheating, which can cause chocolate to seize up into a stiff mass.)

continued from previous page

6. Spoon the melted chocolate into a ziplock bag. Seal the bag, pressing out any air. Use a toothpick to make a tiny hole in one corner of the bag to release a very thin stream of chocolate for writing.

7. To make the spiderwebs, spread white royal icing smoothly over the surface of each cookie. Immediately, before the icing can set, pipe a spiral of chocolate over the surface, starting in the middle and working outward. Starting in the center, use a toothpick to pull outward and inward, alternately, through the icing, making a spider-web design.

Spiderweb Decorating

Whether you're making a spiderweb on a cookie, cake, or cup-cake, you first need to lay down a base of white or dark icing, then pipe out a spiral of a strongly contrasting color on top (such as white icing with a chocolate spiral). Using a toothpick or the tip of a skewer, start at the center of the spiral and pull gently all the way out to the edge. Wipe the tip of the toothpick on a paper towel, and then pull the toothpick from the outside to the center, alternating directions in and out all the way around the circle. (If this makes you nervous, you can also pull out from the center only, but your web won't be quite as complex.)

DEM BONES (OSSI DI MORTI)

This classic Sicilian cookie is traditionally made for All Souls' Day, November 1st (*ossi di morti* is Italian for "bones of the dead"), but nobody will mind if you make them a little in advance for Halloween. The directions call for the cookies to be dried for three days — yes, three days — before baking. You can dry them overnight and still get an acceptable product, but if you bake them sooner they'll spread and darken and you'll think, "These aren't bonelike at all!" Let them dry uncovered as instructed, however, and you'll get unusually crisp and eerily white bones, perfect for dipping in a cup of hot chocolate (or a glass of Italian dessert wine).

2 eggs
2 cups confectioners' sugar
1 cup all-purpose flour

½ teaspoon baking powder
½ teaspoon ground cloves or
1 teaspoon almond extract

1. Beat the eggs in a large bowl with an electric mixer on high speed until thick and lemon-colored, about 5 minutes. Turn the mixer to low and add the confectioners' sugar, beating for another 5 minutes.

2. Combine the flour, baking powder, and cloves in a small bowl, and add to the egg mixture in 4 parts, incorporating each addition fully before adding the next.

3. Turn the dough onto a lightly floured cutting board that you won't need for a few days and shape it into a square about ½ inch thick. Cut the cookies into 36 rectangles, separating them with the knife so that there's 1 inch between them.

4. Leave the cookies to dry, uncovered, at room temperature, for a full 24 hours, or, ideally, up to 3 days.

5. Preheat the oven to 325°F. Grease 2 baking sheets and have ready a small bowl of hot tap water. Dip just the underside of each cookie in the water, leaving the top surface dry, and place on the baking sheet. Bake for 25 minutes, until there's a little pool of golden sugar around each cookie, but the tops are still bone white. Cool completely on the baking sheets. Store in a tightly covered container . . . well, indefinitely.

Makes 24 to 36 cookies, depending on size and shape

Perfect Sugar Cookie Ghosts

If you've been looking for *the* perfect sugar cookie recipe, hunt no more. This one is firm and a bit dry but extremely pliable to work with and the scraps reroll nicely for cutting out more cookies. Best of all, it bakes up into a world-class sugar cookie — smooth and golden, with a wonderful flavor — so don't be tempted to skimp on all that vanilla. It is the ideal rolled dough for making cutouts and can be used for any of the decorative cookies in this chapter (or any other decorative cookies you ever make). Use this dough for any shape you like: I've cut out free-form witch hats, brooms, monster heads, skulls, hands, tombstones, and more.

1 cup (2 sticks) butter, at room temperature
1½ cups confectioners' sugar
1 egg
1 tablespoon vanilla extract
2⅓ cups all-purpose flour
½ teaspoon baking powder
1 recipe Royal Icing (facing page)

1. Beat the butter and sugar in a large mixing bowl until creamy. Add the egg and beat until fluffy. Blend in the vanilla.
2. Sift the flour and baking powder into a small bowl, and then blend into the butter mixture until well combined. Divide the dough in half, wrap each piece in plastic wrap, and chill for 30 minutes. (You can skip this step, but it makes the dough much easier to handle.)
3. Preheat the oven to 350°F and lightly grease 2 baking sheets.
4. On a lightly floured surface, roll out one of the dough halves to a thickness of about ⅛ inch. Use the tip of a paring knife to cut out free-form ghosts (I like a rounded head, no arms, and a tail that curves off to a point, but figure out your ideal Halloween ghost and go with it!). Gather and reroll the scraps. Repeat with the remaining dough half.

5. Carefully lift the cookies with a spatula and transfer them to the prepared baking sheets. Bake for about 8 minutes, until light golden and not at all browned. Cool the cookies completely on the baking sheets before decorating.

6. Use a butter knife to spread royal icing over each cookie. If desired, add candy or chocolate chips for eyes and a mouth.

Royal Icing

Royal icing is extremely versatile; you can divide the amount in this recipe into small cups and tint each portion any color you like to make a decorating buffet for your kids (and yourself).

> 1 **egg white**
> 1 **teaspoon lemon juice**
> 1½ **cups confectioners' sugar**

☠ Whip the egg white and lemon juice in a medium bowl with an electric mixer until frothy. With the mixer on medium, beat in the confectioners' sugar, a little at a time, until the mixture thickens slightly. Turn the mixer to high and continue to beat until the mixture is thick and glossy, about 3 minutes.

☠ Cover the surface with plastic wrap until you're ready to use it. Royal icing will set to a firm, glossy finish when applied to a cookie. The icing can be stored, tightly covered, in the refrigerator for up to 1 week.

LADIES' FINGERS

Red-dyed almonds become manicured fingernails on these particularly eerie fingers. There are lots of variations on Halloween "finger" food (see Witches' Knuckles on page 108), but these look as if they should be starring at a wickedly elegant tea party.

about ½ cup blanched almond
    slices (36 pieces)
red liquid or paste coloring
½ cup (1 stick) butter, at room
    temperature
½ cup confectioners' sugar

¼ cup granulated sugar
1 egg
½ teaspoon vanilla extract
⅛ teaspoon almond extract, optional
½ teaspoon salt
1⅓ cups all-purpose flour

1. Preheat the oven to 350°F and lightly grease a baking sheet.
2. Place the almonds in a disposable plastic container (a yogurt or sour cream cup with a lid, for example), add 8 to 10 drops of liquid coloring or a dab of paste, cover tightly, and shake vigorously. (If you don't have a disposable plastic container, use a ziplock bag and massage well to distribute the color.) Set the almonds on a sheet of wax paper to dry.
3. Cream the butter with the confectioners' sugar and granulated sugar in a large bowl until fluffy. Beat in the egg, vanilla, almond extract, if using, and salt. Blend in the flour. Divide the dough in half, wrap each piece in plastic wrap, and chill for 20 minutes.
4. Preheat the oven to 350°F. Divide one of the dough halves into 18 lumps. Working quickly, roll each one between your palms to form a finger about 4 inches long. Lay it on a baking sheet and squeeze the edges lightly to dent the sides into more of a defined finger shape. Use the blade of a knife to lightly score knuckles. Press a red almond nail, pointed tip out, at the top of each finger.
5. Bake for 8 to 10 minutes, until firm but not at all browned. (The best doneness test is: When you begin to smell cookie in the air, remove the baking sheet from the oven!) Cool completely before storing in an airtight container.

Spooky Shortbread Tombstones

Shortbread tombstones are multipurpose: They look great on a plate, they're delicious, and they're an endlessly useful decoration. Stick them on a cupcake behind a mound of crumbs as a freshly dug grave, make a whole graveyard on a cake (page 79), or pipe the name of a friend on each one, wrap them in cellophane, and use them for place cards at a dinner table or for take-home party favors.

½ cup (1 stick) butter, at room temperature

¼ cup confectioners' sugar

1 cup all-purpose flour

salt

¾ cup semisweet chocolate chips

1. Beat the butter and sugar in a large mixing bowl until smooth and creamy. Add the flour and a pinch of salt and work the mixture with your fingers or a pastry blender until the flour is incorporated. Shape the dough into 2 disks, wrap them separately in plastic wrap, and chill in the refrigerator for 2 to 3 hours.

2. When you're ready to bake, preheat the oven to 325°F. On a lightly floured surface, roll out one disk to a thickness of about ¼ inch. Use a small knife to cut out rectangular or slightly rounded tombstone shapes, 2 to 3 inches tall. Place the cookies on an ungreased baking sheet.

3. Roll and cut the second disk, placing the cookies on a second ungreased baking sheet. Gather and reroll the scraps from both dough disks. Refrigerate the sheets of cookies for 10 minutes.

4. Bake for 15 to 20 minutes, until the shortbread is very lightly golden; do not let the cookies brown. Transfer to a wire rack and cool.

5. When the cookies are completely cool, put the chocolate chips in a microwave-safe bowl and melt the chocolate in the microwave: Heat on high for 60 seconds, and then stir well. If it's not quite smooth, continue to heat in two or three 10-second bursts, stirring well after each burst. (Alternatively, you can melt the chocolate, stirring

frequently, in a double boiler, over just-simmering water. Avoid overheating, which can cause chocolate to seize up into a stiff mass.)

6. Spoon the melted chocolate into a ziplock bag. Seal the bag, pressing out any air. Use a toothpick to make a tiny hole in one corner of the bag to release a thin stream of chocolate for writing. Decorate tombstones with crosses and RIP or other writing as desired. Allow the chocolate to set before stacking the cookies. Store in an airtight container at room temperature for up to 1 week.

Spooky Shortbread Tombstones, as shown on the Whistling Past the Graveyard Cake, page 79

Choco-Bats

These chocolaty bats, formed from a cocoa-enriched dough, are super-dark and rich with butter, as well as being a lot of fun for kids to mold and even more fun to eat. Use red hots to make little red beady eyes or yellow mini M&Ms for glowing orbs.

½ cup (1 stick) butter, at room temperature
½ cup granulated sugar, plus extra for shaping the cookies
½ cup firmly packed brown sugar
1 egg
1 teaspoon vanilla extract

1⅔ cups all-purpose flour
½ cup unsweetened cocoa powder
½ teaspoon baking soda
½ teaspoon salt
mini M&Ms or red hot cinnamon candies

1. Preheat the oven to 350°F and liberally grease 2 baking sheets.
2. Cream the butter, granulated sugar, and brown sugar in a large bowl until fluffy, and then beat in the egg. Stir in the vanilla. Sift in the flour, cocoa, baking soda, and salt, and mix until thoroughly combined.
3. To make a bat, roll two 1-inch balls of dough and place them on a prepared baking sheet. Press each one flat with the bottom of a glass dipped in sugar. Pinch little ears at the top of one of the circles. Cut the other circle in half down the middle with a knife and use the blade to lift and position the 2 halves on either side of the first circle, curved edges down, to make wings. You can also pinch little points along the edge of the wings if you like. Pinch the body edges to the wing edges to make the wings adhere.
4. Put 2 M&Ms or red hots just under the ears to make eyes. Repeat, making 9 bats on each baking sheet, leaving plenty of space in between (because of the way the wings stick out, the bats fit better on the baking sheet if you lay them down at an angle).
5. Bake for 8 to 10 minutes, until set but not browned. Transfer carefully to wire racks and cool completely. Store in an airtight container for up to 1 week.

Swirled Chocolate-Pumpkin Brownies

A dark rich brownie is rarely unwelcome at a party, but these swirled beauties are even better — alongside the buttery chocolate flavor is something more complex: pumpkin and warm spices. These are likely to be a favorite throughout the fall. Try them for dessert, warm, with a scoop of pumpkin ice cream.

½ cup (1 stick) butter	1 cup granulated sugar
6 ounces bittersweet or semisweet baking chocolate, unwrapped and coarsely chopped	½ cup firmly packed brown sugar
	4 eggs
	2 teaspoons vanilla extract
2 cups all-purpose flour	1 (15-ounce) can pumpkin purée (not pumpkin pie filling)
1 teaspoon baking powder	
½ teaspoon salt	¼ cup vegetable oil
1½ teaspoons pumpkin pie spice (page 87)	

1. Preheat the oven to 350°F. Grease a 9-inch square baking pan.

2. Melt the butter and chocolate in a double boiler or in the microwave. Melting chocolate with butter makes it less likely to seize or burn, but check it every 20 seconds and whisk vigorously with a fork. Do not overheat.

3. Combine the flour, baking powder, salt, and pie spice in a medium bowl; set aside.

4. Beat the granulated sugar, brown sugar, eggs, and vanilla with an electric mixer until smooth. Blend in the flour mixture on low speed.

5. Pour half of the batter into a separate bowl and blend the melted chocolate into it. Add the pumpkin and oil to the batter remaining in the mixing bowl.

6. Pour the chocolate batter into the baking pan, then pour the pumpkin batter on top. Working quickly, swirl them gently with a knife, being careful not to overmix. The batters should still look very distinct, with big swirl marks throughout.

7. Bake for 45 minutes, until set. Cool for at least 45 minutes before cutting. Store, tightly covered, for up to 4 days.

CHOCOLATE-CHIP PUMPKIN BARS

The little bit of whole-wheat flour and the pumpkin purée in these moist and tasty bars mean they're practically health food compared to the unrelenting sugar content of most Halloween treats. More important, they're a slightly more grown-up treat — ideal with a cup of coffee — that adults will gladly reach for at any time of day.

1½ cups all-purpose flour
½ cup whole-wheat flour
1 teaspoon baking soda
1 teaspoon salt
2 teaspoons ground cinnamon
1 teaspoon ground ginger
¼ teaspoon ground nutmeg
¼ teaspoon ground cloves
1 cup (2 sticks) butter, at room temperature
1 cup granulated sugar

½ cup firmly packed brown sugar
1 egg
2 teaspoons vanilla extract
1 cup canned pumpkin purée (not pumpkin pie filling)
1 (12-ounce) package semisweet chocolate chips (2 cups)

ORANGE GLAZE
1 cup confectioners' sugar
¼ cup orange juice

1. Preheat the oven to 350°F. Grease a 9- by 13-inch baking pan.

2. Combine the all-purpose flour, whole-wheat flour, baking soda, salt, cinnamon, ginger, nutmeg, and cloves in a medium bowl.

3. Beat the butter, granulated sugar, brown sugar, egg, and vanilla in a large bowl with an electric mixer until smooth. Mix in the pumpkin purée, and then lower the mixer speed and add the flour mixture, beating just until combined.

4. Fold in the chocolate chips and spread the batter in the pan. Bake for 35 minutes, until lightly browned and set.

5. To make the orange glaze, whisk the confectioners' sugar and orange juice in a small bowl. Drizzle the glaze over the cooled bars and cut into squares. Store, tightly covered, for up to 4 days.

CHAPTER 3

CAKES AND CUPCAKES

Cake lends itself well to spooky frosting finishes, whether it's an entire graveyard cake or a writhing sea monster cupcake, rising from the depths and waving around wild marzipan tentacles.

These recipes all begin with homemade cake, but cake mixes are quick and easy, so don't hesitate to substitute your favorite one wherever you like. Don't, however, be tempted to purchase cans of frosting. Homemade frosting is quick and easy, and so much more delicious; it can also be colored any shade to help make your goodies look as fabulous as they taste.

The techniques and treatments that follow are designed to help you make impressive sweets without special decorating tools, so don't hesitate to plunge right in no matter what your experience level is. The biggest problem you might face is finding a serving platter to show off your finished cake. If nothing is quite large enough to hold your 9- by 13-inch graveyard cake, for example, try wrapping a large flat baking sheet in heavy-duty foil, or get a suitable square of lightweight plywood from a lumberyard and wrap it in foil for a sturdy and reusable base. You can surround your cake with fresh and clean fall leaves, or buy cellophane fall leaves at a bake shop, if you're so inclined.

I'SCREAM CAKE

This moist and tender yellow sheet cake has a filling of vanilla ice cream, a thick slather of frosting — and the gaping, mute, horror-stricken face reminiscent of Edvard Munch's iconic painting *The Scream*. Even if you couldn't name the painter for a million bucks, everyone knows the face. The simple, expressive lines are surprisingly easy to recreate in cake and i'scream. If you can, bake the cake in a metal pan — the cake takes a little longer to bake in a glass pan and it is more likely to dry out.

CAKE
- 3 cups all-purpose flour
- 2½ teaspoons baking powder
- 1 teaspoon salt
- ¾ cup (1½ sticks) butter, at room temperature
- 2 cups sugar
- 4 eggs
- 2 teaspoons vanilla extract
- 1 cup whole milk

FROSTING
- ½ cup (1 stick) butter, at room temperature
- 1 (1-pound) package confectioners' sugar (about 4 cups)
- 3-4 tablespoons milk
- 1 teaspoon vanilla extract

FOR ASSEMBLING THE CAKE
- 4 cups (2 pints) vanilla ice cream
- blue liquid or black paste coloring

1. Preheat the oven to 350°F. Grease a 9- by 13-inch metal baking pan and line with parchment or wax paper, leaving a small overhang for lifting the baked cake.

2. Sift the flour, baking powder, and salt into a medium bowl and set aside.

3. Cream the butter and sugar in a large bowl with an electric mixer until fluffy, about 5 minutes. One at a time, beat in the eggs, incorporating each egg well, and then add the vanilla.

4. With the mixer on low, add one-third of the flour mixture, mixing well, and then add one-third of the milk. Repeat twice with the remaining thirds of the flour mixture alternated with the remaining thirds of the milk.

continued from previous page

5. Smooth the batter into the prepared pan and bake for 30 to 35 minutes, until the top is golden and a toothpick inserted in the center comes out with a few crumbs clinging to it. (Try not to overbake; the cake will taste really dry later when it emerges from the freezer.) Cool in the pan for 10 minutes, and then lift the whole cake out with the overhanging edges of parchment and cool completely on a rack.

6. To prepare the frosting, beat the butter in a medium bowl until smooth and creamy. Gradually beat in the confectioners' sugar. Add milk, 1 tablespoon at a time, until the frosting reaches a smooth, spreadable consistency. Stir in the vanilla.

7. To assemble the cake, soften the ice cream on the counter for 10 to 15 minutes, until it's easy to stir and spread but still solid. Peel the paper off the cake and place the cake, top side up, on a serving platter. Using a serrated knife, slice the cake in half horizontally and carefully lift off the top layer and set it aside (it's okay if it breaks — you can put it back together.)

8. Spread the softened ice cream down the length of the cake, and then place the top of the cake back on. Using a serrated knife, trim one end of the cake into a curved shape and trim a slight curve out of each of the long sides, leaving the bottom edge straight and untouched (save trimmings in the freezer for later snacking or trifle-type desserts).

9. Set aside about ⅔ cup of frosting and use the rest to frost the top and sides of the cake, smoothing the top with the back of a knife or a spatula.

10. Color the reserved frosting with the blue or black coloring until you have a dark frosting for drawing a defined outline. Spoon the dark frosting into a ziplock bag and snip off a bit of one bottom corner of the bag. Using the end of a wooden spoon, trace the outline of the face of *The Scream* in the white frosting on the cake — hands clasped to the cheeks, round eyes, and big round mouth in a scream — and then pipe in those lines with the dark frosting. You can make the face fill up the whole cake, or you can leave room to frost in a dark portion of the Screamer's shirt for contrast.

11. Eat at once or, if you must, freeze for up to 2 days. Thaw at room temperature for 20 to 30 minutes before serving (too much longer and the ice cream will melt).

GHOSTLY WHITE CAKE

This very white cake is a suitable background for the fluffy white frosting and the squashy little frosting ghosts dolloped on top, and a nice contrast to the surprise filling. Seven-minute frosting, stabilized with a bit of help from corn syrup or cream of tartar, has just enough body to let each ghost stand up straight if you don't make them too tall. The only color will be from their mournful little chocolate eyes — and the lurid red raspberry jam inside! If you like, sprinkle a thick layer of sweetened, shredded coconut over the top of the cake before you add the ghosts. (Note that you must have a hand-held electric mixer to make the frosting and cake flour to keep the cake white.)

CAKE
- 3 eggs, separated
- 1 cup (2 sticks) butter, at room temperature
- 1½ cups sugar
- 2 teaspoons vanilla extract
- 3 cups cake flour
- 1 tablespoon baking powder
- ½ teaspoon salt
- 1½ cups milk

FROSTING
- 1½ cups sugar
- 1 tablespoon white corn syrup or ¼ teaspoon cream of tartar
- ⅛ teaspoon salt
- ⅓ cup water
- 2 egg whites
- 1½ teaspoons vanilla extract

FOR ASSEMBLING THE CAKE
- 1½ cups (12 ounces) seedless raspberry jam (or other red jam)
- chocolate sprinkles

1. Preheat the oven to 350°F. Grease 3 round 9-inch cake pans and line with parchment or wax paper; grease the paper and set the pans aside.
2. Use an electric mixer to beat the egg whites until they are stiff but not dry. Transfer the beaten egg whites to a medium bowl and set aside. In the used mixing bowl (no need to wash), cream the butter and sugar with the egg yolks until light and fluffy. Beat in the vanilla.

3. Sift the flour, baking powder, and salt into a medium bowl. With the mixer on low, add half of the flour mixture to the butter and sugar. Mix to combine, and then add half of the milk. Repeat with the remaining flour mixture and milk, combining well after each addition. Gently fold in the beaten egg whites with a rubber spatula and divide the batter among the prepared pans.

4. Bake for 18 to 20 minutes, until the cakes just turn a very pale gold and a cake tester or toothpick inserted into the center comes out with a few crumbs clinging to it. Cool in the pans for 10 minutes, and then turn the cakes out onto wire racks to cool completely.

5. To prepare the frosting, bring 1 inch of water to a boil in the bottom of a double boiler. Put the sugar, corn syrup, salt, water, and egg whites in the top section of the double boiler and beat for 1 minute to combine before placing the top section over the inch of boiling water. Watch the clock or set a timer, and beat on high, keeping the water just at a boil over medium heat, for exactly 7 minutes. The frosting will be fluffy, puffy, and white. Remove the pan from the heat (and take the top of the double boiler off the boiling water) and stir in the vanilla.

6. To assemble the cake, place 1 layer on a large serving plate (ideally large enough that you can dollop a few ghosts around the rim of the platter as well as on top of the cake). Briskly stir the jam in a small bowl, and then spread half of it over the bottom layer and top with a dab of frosting. Place the second cake layer on top and spread with the remaining jam and a bit of frosting. Cover with the final layer and frost all over, using about three-quarters of the frosting. Use a spoon to dollop ghosts with the reserved frosting on the top and around the edges of the cake, using the spoon to twist and twirl a head on each one. (You can also pipe ghosts with a round tip on a frosting bag, or through a small hole cut in the corner of a ziplock bag.) Use 2 chocolate sprinkles per ghost to make eyes.

WHISTLING PAST THE GRAVEYARD CAKE

Elaborately decorated sheet cakes are a thrill both to make and to eat, but this one gets even higher marks for being amazingly simple. The finished cake is an extravaganza of chocolate sheet cake with green frosting and piles of chocolate cookie crumbs representing the dirt mound at the foot of each tombstone. The whole graveyard is dotted with marshmallow ghosts and candy pumpkins. Although there's some assembly required, even a first-time cake decorator can achieve a super-professional look because all the parts are so easy. You can turn the cake out onto a large serving platter for a dramatic presentation, or frost and decorate it in the pan for easy transportation if you're taking it to a party.

CAKE
- 2½ cups all-purpose flour
- ½ cup unsweetened cocoa powder
- 1½ teaspoons baking soda
- ½ teaspoon salt
- 1 cup (2 sticks) butter, at room temperature
- 1 cup granulated sugar
- 1 cup firmly packed brown sugar
- 3 eggs
- 2 teaspoons vanilla extract
- 2 cups buttermilk

FROSTING
- 1 cup (2 sticks) butter, at room temperature
- 1 (1-pound) package confectioners' sugar (about 4 cups)
- 3-4 tablespoons milk
- 2 teaspoons vanilla extract
- green liquid or paste coloring

FOR ASSEMBLING THE CAKE
- 6-8 shortbread tombstones (page 64), fully decorated with "RIP," crosses, or names of your friends (you could also use any rectangular cookies with rounded edges — Pepperidge Farm Milanos are just the right shape)
- 5 chocolate sandwich or wafer cookies, crushed to crumbs in a food processor or pounded in a heavy ziplock bag
- candy pumpkins, such as Brach's Mellowcreme Pumpkins
- marshmallows
- mini chocolate chips or M&Ms

continued from previous page

1. Preheat the oven to 350°F. Lightly grease a 9- by 13-inch metal baking pan and set aside.

2. Sift the flour, cocoa, baking soda, and salt into a medium bowl and set aside.

3. Cream the butter, granulated sugar, and brown sugar in a large bowl with an electric mixer until fluffy. One at a time, beat in the eggs, incorporating each egg well, and then add the vanilla. With the mixer on low, add half of the flour mixture and then half of the buttermilk, mixing well after each addition. Repeat with the remaining flour and buttermilk, and then pour the batter into the prepared pan.

4. Bake for 25 to 30 minutes, until a cake tester or toothpick inserted into the center comes out with a few crumbs clinging to it. Cool the cake completely in the pan.

5. To prepare the frosting, beat the butter in a medium bowl until smooth and creamy. Gradually beat in the confectioners' sugar. Add milk, 1 tablespoon at a time, until the frosting reaches a smooth, spreadable consistency. Stir in the vanilla. Tint the frosting a rich green with several drops of liquid coloring or a dab of paste.

6. To decorate the cake, turn it out carefully onto a large serving platter or foil-covered baking sheet, if desired, or leave it in the pan. Spread the frosting over the cake (sides too, if removed from the pan). Stud the top with tombstone cookies. Spoon a generous grave mound of cookie crumbs at the foot of each tombstone, and then nestle candy pumpkins here and there among the graves. Use scissors to snip off the tops of 2 marshmallows and stick the cut sides together to form ghosts. You can also snip the top of the head into a rounded shape. Make 2 little cuts in the heads and tuck in chocolate sprinkles or mini chocolate chips for eyes.

Super Grass

If you have a pastry bag and a set of cake decorating tips, it's easy to make this cake look much more elaborate by using any of the finest (smallest) tips to pipe little blades of grass all over the top. It's easy — just point and squeeze, point and squeeze to make individual grass blades all over the surface.

WITCH'S HAT SHEET CAKE

With a little ingenuity and a couple of extra blobs of frosting to fill in the gaps, you can turn a simple rectangular chocolate sheet cake into a very impressive — and sizable — triangular witch's hat that will have every child in the room oohing and aahing. Add to that the cake's covering of gleaming, buttery, chocolate frosting with a wide green frosting band and a jolly purple frosting buckle, and you have a cake that will have people cackling with joy.

CAKE

- 1 cup all-purpose flour
- ⅓ cup unsweetened cocoa powder
- 1 teaspoon baking soda
- ½ teaspoon salt
- ½ cup (1 stick) butter, at room temperature
- ½ cup granulated sugar
- ½ cup firmly packed brown sugar
- 2 eggs
- 1 teaspoon vanilla extract
- 1 cup buttermilk

FROSTING

- ½ cup (1 stick) butter, at room temperature
- 1 (1-pound) package confectioners' sugar (about 4 cups)
- 3-4 tablespoons milk or cream
- 1 teaspoon vanilla extract
  red, blue, and green liquid coloring or green and purple paste coloring
- ⅓ cup unsweetened cocoa powder

1. Preheat the oven to 350°F. Lightly grease an 11- by 15- by 1-inch rimmed baking sheet (what my mother called a "jelly roll pan") and set aside.

2. Sift the flour, cocoa, baking soda, and salt into a medium bowl and set aside.

3. Cream the butter, granulated sugar, and brown sugar in a large bowl with an electric mixer until fluffy. One at a time, beat in the eggs, incorporating each egg well, and then add the vanilla.

4. With the mixer on low, add half of the flour mixture and then half of the buttermilk, mixing well after each addition. Repeat with the remaining flour and buttermilk, and then pour the batter into the prepared pan.

continued from previous page

5. Bake for 18 to 20 minutes, until a cake tester or toothpick inserted in the center comes out with a few crumbs clinging to it. Don't overbake. Cool the cake in the pan while you color the frosting.

6. To prepare the frosting, beat the butter in a medium bowl until smooth and creamy. Gradually beat in the confectioners' sugar. Add milk, 1 tablespoon at a time, until the frosting reaches a smooth, spreadable consistency. Stir in the vanilla.

7. Remove ¼ cup of the frosting to a small bowl and color it green with a dab of paste or a few drops of liquid coloring. Remove another ½ cup of white frosting to a different bowl and color it purple with a dab of paste or with a few drops each of blue and red liquid coloring. Set the 2 bowls of colored frosting aside.

8. Mix the cocoa with the remaining frosting and beat until smooth, adding more confectioners' sugar and 1 teaspoon or more of milk or cream, if necessary, to achieve a smooth spreading consistency.

9. Unmold the cake onto a large serving platter. Use a serrated knife to cut 2 long triangles off the long sides of the cake and carefully lift them, using a long offset spatula or the blade of the knife as a support. Move the cut pieces to the bottom sides of the cake to form the brim of the heat, with the narrow ends of the long triangles pointing out to the edges. The triangles may not fit perfectly like a puzzle, but push them firmly up against the sides of the cake as closely as possible — a soft, slightly warm cake is easier to gently mold than a cooled one.

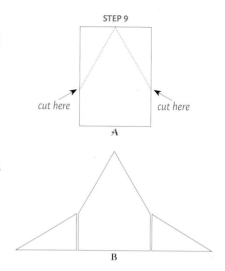

10. Frost the entire cake with the chocolate frosting, filling in the gaps around the brim with extra frosting. Allow the frosted cake to set for 10 minutes, then use a butter knife to make a 4-inch-wide hat band of green frosting straight across the bottom of the triangular part of the hat, just above the brim.

11. Spoon the purple frosting into a small ziplock bag and cut off the tip of one corner. Pipe the outline of a large square "buckle" to one side of the band, extending into the chocolate frosting on both sides, and then widen the outline of the buckle so it's a hollow square whose walls are about 1 inch wide, with the green of the hat band visible in the center. Store, tightly covered, for 4 to 5 days.

PUMPKIN SPICE JACK-O'-LANTERN CAKE

Impressive but surprisingly easy, this jack-o'-lantern requires two full cake recipes baked in a Bundt pan — plenty of cake for a big party! You must mix each batch separately rather than doubling the recipe. You can unmold the first cake and bake a second right away, or you can bake one cake earlier and freeze it for later use. (Cool it completely and double-wrap it in foil and plastic wrap for freezing.) The moist pumpkin batter yields a fresh-tasting cake, even after the freezer stint.

FOR EACH CAKE
- 3 cups all-purpose flour
- 2 teaspoons baking powder
- ½ teaspoon baking soda
- ½ teaspoon salt
- 2 teaspoons pumpkin pie spice (page 87)
- ½ cup (1 stick) butter, at room temperature
- 1 cup granulated sugar
- 1 cup firmly packed brown sugar
- 4 eggs
- 1 tablespoon vanilla extract
- ½ cup sour cream
- 1 (15-ounce) can pumpkin purée (not pumpkin pie filling)
- ½ cup chopped walnuts, optional

CREAM CHEESE FROSTING
- 1 (8-ounce) package cream cheese, at room temperature
- ½ cup (1 stick) butter, at room temperature
- 5 cups confectioners' sugar
- 2-4 tablespoons milk
- 2 teaspoons vanilla extract
  green liquid or paste coloring
  red and yellow liquid coloring or orange paste coloring

FOR ASSEMBLING THE CAKE
- ½ cup semisweet chocolate chips

1. Preheat the oven to 350°F. Grease and flour a Bundt pan and line one 4-ounce ramekin or custard cup with a muffin paper.

2. Sift the flour, baking powder, baking soda, salt, and pumpkin pie spice into a large bowl and set aside.

continued from previous page

3. Cream the butter, granulated sugar, and brown sugar in a large bowl with an electric mixer until fluffy. One at a time, beat the eggs into the mixture, and then blend in the vanilla, sour cream, and pumpkin, mixing to combine. Add the egg mixture to the dry ingredients in halves, mixing until smooth. Stir in the walnuts, if using.

4. Scoop out ⅓ cup of the batter and pour it into the paper-lined ramekin. Pour the remaining batter into the Bundt pan. Place both pans in the oven; remove the ramekin after 15 minutes. Continue baking the Bundt cake for 30 to 35 minutes longer, until a toothpick comes out with only a few crumbs clinging to it.

5. Make an entire second cake by repeating steps 1 through 3. Skip the small ramekin cake and pour all of the batter into the prepared Bundt pan. Bake 45 to 50 minutes and cool the second cake.

6. To prepare the frosting, beat the cream cheese and butter in a large bowl until smooth and creamy. Slowly blend in the confectioners' sugar. Add milk, 1 tablespoon at a time, until the frosting achieves a smooth, spreadable consistency. Stir in the vanilla.

7. Remove ½ cup of the frosting to a small bowl and blend in about 6 drops of the green coloring (add a few drops more if you want a more intense shade). Stir about 10 drops each of the red and yellow coloring or a dab of the orange paste into the remaining white frosting to produce a bright orange.

8. When both Bundt cakes are entirely cool, place the slightly larger Bundt cake (the second one) upside down on a serving platter (the rounded edge of the cake will be on the bottom). Spread a thin layer of orange frosting over the flat side as a glue, and then place the second cake right side up directly on top of the first, making sure to line up the ridges.

9. Frost the cake assembly evenly with orange frosting. Peel the paper off the little cupcake from the ramekin and frost its bottom and sides with the bright green frosting. Place it, top side down and frosted bottom up, in the center of the top Bundt cake, covering the hole, to make a pumpkin stem. (You can use a knife to smooth away your fingerprints from placing the cupcake.)

10. Put the chocolate chips in a microwave-safe bowl, and melt the chocolate in the microwave: Heat on high for 60 seconds, and then stir well. If it's not quite smooth, continue to heat in two or three 10-second bursts, stirring well after each burst. Cool slightly, then pour the melted chocolate into a small ziplock bag. Cut a tiny bit off one corner of the bag and pipe a triangular nose and eyes high up on one side of the cake, then a jagged pumpkin grin. (You get only one shot at this on the cake so you may want to melt extra chips and practice on a piece of wax paper or a plate first.) Serve immediately, or store, covered, for 2 to 3 days.

Makes about ¼ cup

Make Your Own Pumpkin Pie Spice

There's no secret to pumpkin pie spice, which is a premixed convenience for the autumn cook. If I want a more intense ginger or nutmeg flavor, for example, I might measure out each spice separately in a recipe. Don't bother buying premixed spice if you already have these five basic flavors in your cupboard: here's a recipe to make your own. Grate your own nutmeg to give a much fresher and more pungent flavor to the finished mix.

2 tablespoons ground cinnamon	1½ teaspoons ground allspice
1 tablespoon ground ginger	¾ teaspoon ground cloves
1½ teaspoons ground nutmeg	

☠ Combine spices and use in any recipe calling for pumpkin pie spice. Store in a tightly closed jar.

SPIDERY CUPCAKES

Red velvet cupcakes are a luscious base for these leggy, spidery cupcakes. Frosting the cupcakes white and using red licorice keep these spiders lighthearted and goofy. If you want darker, scarier cupcakes, beat cocoa into the frosting and use black licorice.

RED VELVET CUPCAKES
1¾ **cups all-purpose flour**
2 **tablespoons unsweetened cocoa powder**
1½ **teaspoons baking soda**
1 **teaspoon salt**
¾ **cup vegetable oil**
1 **cup sugar**
1 **cup buttermilk**
2 **eggs**
2 **tablespoons red liquid coloring**
1 **teaspoon vanilla extract**

CREAM CHEESE FROSTING
1 **(8-ounce) package cream cheese, at room temperature**
½ **cup (1 stick) butter, at room temperature**
6 **cups confectioners' sugar**
1 **teaspoon vanilla extract**
½ **cup unsweetened cocoa powder, optional (see headnote)**

FOR ASSEMBLING THE CUPCAKES
red licorice strings (or twisted licorice ropes that you can unwind)
chocolate sprinkles
mini-marshmallows or red hots

1. Preheat the oven to 350°F. Line two 12-cup muffin tins with paper liners.
2. Sift the flour, cocoa powder, baking soda, and salt into a medium bowl, and set aside.
3. Beat the oil, sugar, and buttermilk in a large bowl with an electric mixer until blended. Add the eggs, red coloring, and vanilla, and mix well. With the mixer on low, add the flour mixture a little at a time, scraping down the sides occasionally. Mix just until combined. Spoon the batter into the liners, filling them halfway.
4. Bake for 16 to 18 minutes, until a toothpick inserted into the center of a cupcake comes out with a few crumbs clinging to it. Cool in the pans for 10 minutes, and then turn the cupcakes out onto racks to cool completely.

continued from previous page

5. To prepare the frosting, beat the cream cheese and butter in a large bowl with an electric mixer until smooth. Gradually add the confectioners' sugar and beat until the frosting reaches a smooth, spreadable consistency. Stir in the vanilla. Beat in the cocoa powder, if desired.

6. Frost the cooled cupcakes generously. To make spiders, insert 8 dangly licorice legs around a cupcake, and shower a tablespoon of sprinkles on top. Put 2 mini-marshmallows on the front edge for eyes. Dip the tips of 2 chocolate sprinkles in frosting and stick 1 sprinkle to each marshmallow eye to make a pupil. Or use red hots to make spooky little glowing eyes. (To make bigger, scarier spiders, use thick black licorice and cut halfway through each twist to make a leg joint. Stick the legs into the cupcake and let the ends touch the platter. These work better with 6 legs instead of the requisite 8. Store, tightly covered, for up to 4 days.

TOMBSTONE CUPCAKES

Each tasty and moist devil's food cupcake is a tiny grave, with a mound of dirt, a tombstone, and a pumpkin, for good measure, on top. But what's in the grave? Buried in each cupcake is a miniature peanut butter cup! If you don't want to make shortbread tombstones specifically for this recipe, you can use any rectangular cookie with a rounded edge, such as Pepperidge Farms Milanos, or you can make a few tombstone shapes out of any other cookie dough you're baking, such as the Choco-Bats (page 66).

CUPCAKES
- 1¾ cups all-purpose flour
- ⅓ cup unsweetened cocoa powder
- 1½ teaspoons baking soda
- ¼ teaspoon salt
- ½ cup (1 stick) butter, at room temperature
- 1 cup granulated sugar
- ½ cup firmly packed brown sugar
- 2 eggs
- 1½ teaspoons vanilla extract
- 1½ cups buttermilk
- 18 miniature peanut butter cups, unwrapped

FROSTING
- ½ cup (1 stick) butter, at room temperature
- 1 (1-pound) package confectioners' sugar (about 4 cups)
- 3–4 tablespoons milk
- 1 teaspoon vanilla extract
  green liquid or paste coloring

FOR ASSEMBLING THE CUPCAKES
- 18 tombstone cookies (page 64)
- 5 chocolate sandwich cookies, crushed into crumbs
- 18 candy pumpkins, optional

1. Preheat the oven to 350°F. Line 18 cups in two 12-cup muffin tins with paper liners.
2. Sift the flour, cocoa, baking soda, and salt into a medium bowl and set aside.
3. Cream the butter, granulated sugar, and brown sugar in a large bowl with an electric mixer until fluffy. One at a time, beat in the eggs, incorporating each egg well, and then add the vanilla. With the mixer on low, add half of the flour mixture and then half of the buttermilk, beating until blended. Add the remaining flour and then the remaining buttermilk, beating until combined.

continued from previous page

4. Spoon the batter into the liners, filling them no more than two-thirds full. Press a peanut butter cup into the center of each cupcake, burying it in the batter.

5. Bake for 18 minutes, until a toothpick inserted into the center of a cupcake comes out with a few crumbs clinging to it. Cool in the pans for 10 minutes, and then turn the cupcakes out onto racks to cool completely.

6. To prepare the frosting, beat the butter in a medium bowl until smooth and creamy. Gradually beat in the confectioners' sugar. Add milk, 1 tablespoon at a time, until the frosting reaches a smooth, spreadable consistency. Stir in the vanilla. Mix in the coloring to get a lurid, grassy green.

7. Frost the cooled cupcakes generously. If you have a pastry bag, you can use a fine tip to pipe blades of grass on the surface. Place an upright tombstone in the center of each cupcake, spoon some cookie crumbs at its base, and nestle a pumpkin next to the tombstone, if desired. Store, tightly covered, for up to 4 days.

WORMY CUPCAKES

Tender yellow cupcakes with a delectable milk chocolate frosting seem simple enough — until you realize they have a little worm problem. Heaps of gummy worms dangling from the frosting will delight children, but may encourage the adults at your party to take a pass.

CUPCAKES

1¾ cups all-purpose flour
1½ teaspoons baking powder
¼ teaspoon salt
½ cup (1 stick) butter, at room
   temperature
1 cup sugar
2 eggs
1 teaspoon vanilla extract
½ cup milk

FROSTING

1 cup milk chocolate chips
4 cups confectioners' sugar
¼ cup milk
4 tablespoons butter, at room
   temperature
2 teaspoons vanilla extract
¼ teaspoon salt

FOR ASSEMBLING THE CUPCAKES

8 chocolate sandwich cookies, such
   as Oreos, processed to crumbs
   in a food processor
gummy worms

1. Preheat the oven to 350°F. Line 18 cups in two 12-cup muffin tins with paper liners.

2. Sift the flour, baking powder, and salt into a medium bowl and set aside.

3. Beat the butter and sugar in a large bowl with an electric mixer until light and fluffy, about 3 minutes. One at a time, beat in the eggs, incorporating each egg well, and then add the vanilla. With the mixer on low, add half of the flour mixture and then all of the milk, beating just until combined. Add the rest of the flour and mix until combined. Spoon the batter into the liners, filling them halfway.

4. Bake for 16 to 18 minutes, until a toothpick inserted into the center of a cupcake comes out clean. Cool in the pans for 10 minutes, and then turn the cupcakes out onto racks to cool completely.

5. To prepare the frosting, put the chocolate chips in a microwave-safe bowl, and melt the chocolate in the microwave: Heat on high in 10-second bursts, stirring well after each burst. (Alternatively, you can melt the chocolate, stirring frequently, in a double boiler, over just-simmering water. Avoid overheating, which can cause chocolate to seize up into a stiff mass.) Add the confectioners' sugar, milk, butter, vanilla, and salt to the chocolate, and beat with an electric mixer until creamy.

6. Frost the cooled cupcakes generously, and then poke 4 gummy worms into the frosting, some coiled on top and others dangling over the side. Store, tightly covered, for up to 4 days.

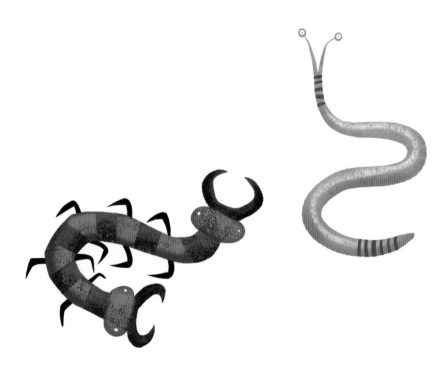

MONSTER CUPCAKES

Paste coloring and marshmallows make for lurid green monsters with chocolate hair in these enticing little Frankenstein cakes. They have a spicy pumpkin-gingerbread cupcake hidden underneath.

CUPCAKES
- 1½ cups all-purpose flour
- 1 teaspoon baking powder
- ¼ teaspoon salt
- 2 teaspoons pumpkin pie spice (page 87)
- ½ cup (1 stick) butter, at room temperature
- ¾ cup sugar
- 2 eggs
- ½ cup canned pumpkin purée (not pumpkin pie filling)
- ½ cup buttermilk
- 1 teaspoon vanilla extract

FOR ASSEMBLING THE CUPCAKES
- 1 recipe Cream Cheese Frosting (page 89)
  green paste coloring
- 18 marshmallows
- 1 cup semisweet chocolate chips
- 18 pretzel sticks
  chocolate sprinkles, or other candy as desired, for faces

1. Preheat the oven to 350°F. Line 18 cups in two 12-cup muffin tins with paper liners.
2. Sift the flour, baking powder, salt, and pumpkin pie spice into a medium bowl and set aside.
3. Beat the butter and sugar in a large bowl with an electric mixer until smooth and creamy. One at a time, beat in the eggs, incorporating each egg well, and then blend in the pumpkin, buttermilk, and vanilla. With the mixer on low, add the flour mixture and blend just until combined. Spoon the batter into the liners.

continued from previous page

4. Bake for 18 to 20 minutes, until a toothpick inserted into the center of a cupcake comes out clean. Cool in the pans for 10 minutes, and then turn the cupcakes out onto racks to cool completely.

5. Color the cream cheese frosting light green with paste coloring. Reserve 1½ cups of frosting and frost the cupcakes with the rest.

6. Holding each marshmallow by its flat ends, roll the rounded sides in the remaining frosting to coat and color them green. Set on a plate to dry while you melt the chocolate chips in the microwave in 10-second bursts, stirring after each burst. (Alternatively, you can melt the chocolate, stirring frequently, in a double boiler over just-simmering water. Avoid overheating, which can cause chocolate to seize up into a stiff mass.)

7. Dip the top (a flat end) of each marshmallow in chocolate to make "hair." Break a pretzel stick in half and stick one on either side of the marshmallow's "neck." Using another pretzel stick as a paintbrush, make chocolate dots for eyes and a straight line for a mouth, or use the melted chocolate to stick sprinkles or other candy on the front to make a face. Set the finished head on top of the cupcake. Store, tightly covered, for up to 4 days.

Hairy Eye Cupcakes

Despite being decorated to look like an eyeball, these yellow cupcakes are elegantly good-looking, with a piped frame of stylized chocolate eyelashes around a gleaming red gumdrop eyeball and a road map of red frosting veins.

CUPCAKES
1¾ cups all-purpose flour
1½ teaspoons baking powder
¼ teaspoon salt
½ cup (1 stick) butter, at room temperature
1 cup sugar
2 eggs
1 teaspoon vanilla extract
½ cup milk

FROSTING
½ cup (1 stick) butter, at room temperature
1 (1-pound) package confectioners' sugar (about 4 cups)
3–4 tablespoons milk
1 teaspoon vanilla extract
red liquid or paste coloring

FOR ASSEMBLING THE CUPCAKES
18 gumdrops or jelly beans
¾ cup semisweet chocolate chips

1. Preheat the oven to 350°F. Line 18 cups in two 12-cup muffin tins with paper liners.

2. Sift the flour, baking powder, and salt into a medium bowl and set aside.

3. Beat the butter and sugar in a large bowl with an electric mixer until light and fluffy, about 3 minutes. One at a time, beat in the eggs, incorporating each egg well, and then add the vanilla. With the mixer on low, add half of the flour mixture and then all of the milk, beating just until combined. Add the rest of the flour and mix until combined. Spoon the batter into the liners, filling them halfway.

4. Bake for 16 to 18 minutes, until a toothpick inserted into the center of a cupcake comes out clean. Cool in the pans for 10 minutes, and then turn the cupcakes out onto racks to cool completely.

continued from previous page

5. To prepare the frosting, beat the butter in a medium bowl until smooth and creamy. Gradually beat in the confectioners' sugar. Add milk, 1 tablespoon at a time, until the frosting reaches a smooth, spreadable consistency. Stir in the vanilla.

6. Spoon ¾ cup of the frosting into a small bowl and color it dark red. Spoon the red frosting into a ziplock bag and set aside. Frost the cupcakes with the remaining white frosting, leaving a ¼-inch unfrosted ring around the outer edges of the cupcakes. Put a gumdrop or jelly bean in the center of each.

7. Put the chocolate chips in a microwave-safe bowl, and melt the chocolate in the microwave: Heat on high for 60 seconds, and then stir well. If it's not quite smooth, continue to heat in two or three 10-second bursts, stirring well after each burst. (Alternatively, you can melt the chocolate, stirring frequently, in a double boiler, over just-simmering water. Avoid overheating, which can cause chocolate to seize up into a stiff mass.) Pour the chocolate into a ziplock bag. Poke a hole in one corner of the bag with a toothpick and pipe eyelashes all around the frosted white centers.

8. Poke a hole in one corner of the red frosting bag with a toothpick and pipe red squiggles away from the pupil in each eye to make veins. Store, tightly covered, for up to 4 days.

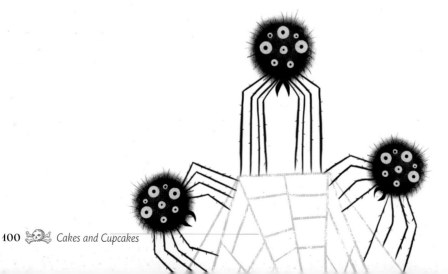

CREATURE FEATURE CUPCAKES

These alarming sea monsters, with waving tentacles and a single, staring eye, require a bit more effort than the other goodies in the book, but if you're feeling crafty, children are delighted by these green frights. The tentacles are made from purchased marzipan, an almond paste available in the baking section of most supermarkets. Marzipan provides a sort of ready-to-eat play dough that you can color green by kneading in paste coloring. I strongly recommend paste coloring when working with marzipan — liquid color will change the texture and the marzipan tentacles won't stand up correctly on top of the cupcake.

CUPCAKES

- 1¼ cups all-purpose flour
- 1 teaspoon baking soda
- ¼ teaspoon salt
- 2 teaspoons pumpkin pie spice (page 87)
- ½ cup (1 stick) butter, at room temperature
- ½ cup sugar
- ½ cup molasses
- 1 egg
- ½ cup hot milk

FOR ASSEMBING THE CUPCAKES

- 1 recipe Cream Cheese Frosting (page 85)
  green paste coloring
- 12 orange or lemon gummy fruit slices
- 12 chocolate-covered sunflower seeds
- 2 (7-ounce) cans marzipan
  pearl or silver dragees

1. Preheat the oven to 350°F. Line one 12-cup muffin tin with paper liners.
2. Sift the flour, baking soda, salt, and pumpkin pie spice into a medium bowl and set aside.
3. Beat the butter and sugar in a large bowl until light and creamy. Beat in the molasses and the egg. Add the flour mixture and stir just until combined and then blend in the milk. Spoon the batter into the liners.

continued from previous page

4. Bake for 16 to 18 minutes, until a toothpick inserted into the center of a cupcake comes out clean. Cool in the pans for 10 minutes, and then turn the cupcakes out onto racks to cool completely.

5. Color the cream cheese frosting green with a dab of paste coloring. Put the frosting in a pastry bag fitted with a plain, midsize tip (such as a U7 tube), pipe the icing on top in wide, concentric circles, starting at the outside and spiraling inward to a slightly domed center, like a coiled rope. (You can also use a ziplock bag with one corner cut off, but your coil won't be quite as evenly rounded.)

6. Use a bit of frosting to stick a chocolate-covered sunflower seed in the middle of each gummy fruit slice and set them aside.

Rolling Marzipan

Because marzipan is sticky and may tear if handled too roughly, it helps to follow a few simple steps:

1. Wet a clean dish towel, wring it out, and lay it flat on the counter.

2. Place a large sheet of wax paper directly on the wet cloth.

3. Lay the marzipan disk on the wax paper and cover with a second large sheet of wax paper.

4. Roll firmly but gently. The wet towel will prevent the wax paper from slipping on the surface. If the top sheet wrinkles as you roll, keep pulling it smooth so the marzipan beneath won't wrinkle.

5. To cut the marzipan, place it, still sandwiched between the 2 sheets of wax paper, on a cutting board. Lift off the top sheet and cut the tentacles out directly on the wax paper.

---

7. Set up a stain-proof work surface, such as a large, flat platter or a large sheet of parchment, and, wearing latex gloves to protect your hands from the coloring, knead the marzipan until it becomes softened and malleable. Make a dent on the surface and dab on some green paste. Knead the color through the marzipan, adding more as necessary to achieve a lurid shade, and pat the marzipan into 4 disks about 3 inches in diameter.

8. Use a rolling pin to roll each disk out to a thickness of ¼ inch. With the tip of a sharp knife, cut each disk into 12 triangles 3 to 4 inches long and about ¾ inch wide at the base. Press dragees all over one side of each triangle.

9. Stick a gummy fruit slice, rounded edge up, in the center of each cupcake.

10. Using the blade of a knife or an offset spatula to lift the marzipan triangles from the cutting board, place 4 tentacles on each cupcake, around and behind the fruit slice eye, curling and twisting each tentacle downward as you place it (the dragees should be on the underside of each curl).

11. These are best eaten within 24 hours, before your tentacles begin to droop, but they can be stored, tightly covered, for up to 4 days.

CHAPTER 4

PARTY FOOD, SNACKS, AND DRINKS

Party food for Halloween walks a fine line between being thrilling and being too yucky to eat. You can have the most delicious dish in the world, but if it looks too much like body parts, for example, people may admire, but not eat, your hard work. So be aware when you're making party food that tastiness ought to trump creepiness so that nobody goes home hungry.

But that doesn't mean that you can't have fun. A mound of Cheddar Eyeballs or a heap of Witches' Knuckles on a platter make it abundantly clear what holiday is being celebrated, and yet these savory, cheesy pastries, warm from the oven, are also an ideal accompaniment to a cold grown-up drink.

The best Halloween party food is spooky and delicious — from spicy hot chocolate with marshmallow ghosts melting into the surface to a pumpkin cheesecake with a spider-web decorating the top.

WITCHES' KNUCKLES

These gnarled nibbles, with their pepperoni fingernails and rosemary knuckles, are extremely tasty. It's possible to make slightly more desiccated and gnarled fingers, but they won't taste as good as these spicy, cheesy digits, which are made with a choux pastry, the same tender dough used to make éclairs.

1 cup water
½ cup (1 stick) butter
1 cup all-purpose flour
1 teaspoon salt
1 teaspoon ground cumin
1 teaspoon chili powder
4 eggs
1 tablespoon Dijon mustard

4 ounces extra-sharp cheddar
   cheese, grated (about 1 cup)
1 egg yolk, lightly beaten with
   1 tablespoon water
   dried whole rosemary leaves
9 pieces of sliced pepperoni, cut
   into quarters

1. Preheat the oven to 400°F. Line 2 baking sheets with parchment or wax paper.
2. Place the water and butter in a saucepan and bring to a boil over medium heat. Take the pan off the heat and stir in the flour, salt, cumin, and chili powder. Return the mixture to the heat and cook, beating constantly with a wooden spoon until the dough starts to pull away from the sides of the pan, 1 to 2 minutes.
3. Remove from the heat and stir for 1 to 2 minutes, until slightly cooled. One at a time, beat in the eggs, incorporating each egg well. Stir in the mustard and cheese.
4. Put the dough in a ziplock bag and cut a ½-inch hole in one corner. Squeeze 3-inch-long fingers onto the prepared baking sheets. Brush them with the egg yolk mixture and press a pepperoni fingernail onto each tip. Lay a few rosemary needles just beneath the nail and in the middle of the finger as knuckle lines.
5. Bake for 15 to 18 minutes, until the fingers are golden brown and crisp. Serve hot or warm. If you store them (in a sealed bag in the refrigerator for up to 3 days), reheat for 6 to 8 minutes in a 350°F oven before serving.

BANDAGED FINGERS

Pigs in blankets take on a whole new look when they have a fingernail at one end and a bandage of flour tortilla wrapped around. A dab of ketchup on the tip makes them extra spooky. Serve with more ketchup or a dish of mustard for dipping.

> 36 **cocktail weiners**
> 6 **large flour tortillas**
> **ketchup**

1. Preheat the oven to 350°F. With a sharp paring knife, trim a wide, flat, 45-degree cut from one end of each weiner to make a fingernail.

2. Slice each tortilla into 6 strips about an inch wide and wrap 1 strip around each finger, starting just below the cut.

3. Place the fingers on a baking sheet with the loose edges tucked underneath and put a dollop of ketchup on each nail. Bake for 10 minutes, until hot and lightly browned.

CHEDDAR EYEBALLS

These cheesy, salty bites with a glaring eyeball in each make an excellent accompaniment to adult cocktails, if your party swings more toward adults, but kids love them too. The dough puffs when it bakes so don't shape them too big.

8 ounces extra-sharp cheddar
   cheese, grated (about 2 cups)
½ cup (1 stick) butter, cut into
   6 pieces
1 teaspoon ground cumin

½ teaspoon salt
1 cup all-purpose flour
1 (6-ounce) bottle pimento-stuffed
   green olives, drained

1. Preheat the oven to 400°F.
2. Combine the cheese, butter, cumin, and salt in a food processor and process until well blended. With the machine running, slowly add the flour and stop as soon as a ball of dough forms.
3. Scoop up a tablespoon of the cheese dough and mold it into a ball. Push an olive down into the middle of the eyeball, leaving only the stuffed end showing. Place on an ungreased baking sheet. Repeat with the remaining dough and olives.
4. Bake for 12 to 15 minutes, until golden brown. Serve hot or warm.

PUMPKIN SEEDS, SPICY AND SWEET

When you carve your jack-o'-lantern, don't throw away the guts! Those seeds are snacking gold, whether you make them sweet or spicy. Both varieties will keep for one week in an airtight container.

SPICY
- 2 cups pumpkin seeds, picked clear of pulp and rinsed
- 2 tablespoons olive oil
- 1 teaspoon kosher salt
- ¼ teaspoon cayenne pepper
- several dashes Worcestershire sauce

1. Preheat the oven to 325°F. Pat the seeds dry with paper towels.
2. Toss the pumpkin seeds with the oil, salt, cayenne, and Worcestershire in a medium bowl. Spread them on a rimmed baking sheet and roast for about 25 minutes, shaking the pan occasionally, until browned and crunchy. Serve warm or at room temperature.

SWEET
- 2 cups pumpkin seeds, rinsed and picked clear of pulp
- 2 tablespoons olive oil
- ½ teaspoon salt
- 1 tablespoon butter
- ⅓ cup sugar
- ½ teaspoon pumpkin pie spice (page 87)

1. Preheat the oven to 325°F. Pat the seeds dry with paper towels.
2. Toss the pumpkin seeds with the oil and salt in a medium bowl. Spread them on a rimmed baking sheet and roast for about 25 minutes, as described above.
3. Melt the butter in a large skillet over medium heat. Stir in 2 tablespoons of the sugar and cook, stirring, for 2 to 3 minutes, until the sugar begins to melt. Add the toasted pumpkin seeds and stir to combine with the melted sugar. Remove the pan from the heat and sprinkle with the remaining sugar and pumpkin pie spice and toss to combine. Pour onto a wax-paper-lined platter to cool a bit (the sugar will be hot), and serve warm or at room temperature.

BITE-YOUR-TONGUE SPICED CIDER

Heady with spice and fragrant with orange zest, this apple cider screams "autumn." Holding a toasty cupful is the perfect way to warm little fingers that may have gotten chilled on trick-or-treating rounds. The longer you let the spices mellow in the pot, the more flavorful your cider will be.

- 1 **gallon apple cider**
- 2 **oranges**
- 12 **cinnamon sticks**
- 1 **tablespoon cardamom pods**
- 1 **teaspoon whole cloves**

1. Pour the cider into a large pot. Peel the zest off the oranges in long strips using a sharp paring knife or a vegetable peeler. Cut the oranges in half and squeeze the juice into the cider, being careful not to include the seeds. Add the zest, cinnamon sticks, cardamom, and cloves to the pot.

2. Bring to a simmer over medium-high heat. Stir and cook for about 5 minutes. Keep the cider warm over very low heat and discard spices and zest as you serve.

SCREAMING RED PUNCH WITH A HAND

A frozen hand in punch is a Halloween standard because it always looks terrific, even if you have already seen it dozens of times as a child. Use a surgical or thin, disposable latex glove (you can buy them in the housewares department of any big-box store) or even a rubber housework glove. To transfer your frozen hand out of the glove and into the punch bowl intact, you must cut the glove off the palm and each finger with sharp scissors — it will not roll off in one piece.

- 1 **new rubber surgical glove**
- 2 **quarts apple juice**
- 2 **quarts cranberry juice (cranberry-pomegranate is nice too)**
- 2 **liters ginger ale**

1. Rinse the glove inside and out several times with cold water to make sure it doesn't have any powder coating. Fill with water and tie the wrist tightly closed with a twist tie. Freeze solid.

2. Mix the juices and ginger ale in a large punch bowl. Cut the glove carefully off the hand and fingers with a sharp scissors and float the molded hand in the punch.

GHOUL-ADE WITH FLY-IN-MY-ICE

The combination of grape and orange Kool-Aid results in a punch that's aggressively black in color and unidentifiably fruity in taste. The addition of ginger ale adds a bit of zing, and the fun comes from ice cubes frozen with a raisin inside. Drop them into the black punch and they look for all the world like flies trapped in ice. If the punch is well chilled before serving, the fly ice will last longer.

12 raisins
2 packages unsweetened grape Kool-Aid
1 package unsweetened orange Kool-Aid
2 cups sugar
3 quarts very cold water
1 liter very cold ginger ale

1. One day before your party, fill a 12-cube ice cube tray with water and drop a raisin in each. Freeze solid.
2. Mix the Kool-Aid with sugar and water and then pour in the ginger ale. Unmold the ice cubes and drop in just before serving.

Waiter, There's a Fly in My Ice

Show off your raisin flies to their best advantage in super-clear ice cubes, made from boiled water. Cool the boiled water before filling the ice trays and dropping in your raisins. It's a bit of extra work, but the result will be translucent.

If you're going the extra mile, mix up your Kool-Aid the day before and freeze a couple cups of it in some small rounded containers (such as teacups) and use those for ice as well as the "fly ice." The Kool-Aid ice will not dilute your punch as it melts.

If you don't have a suitable punch bowl, serve your ghoulish concoction in a large mixing or salad bowl, a stockpot, or even a new plastic basin. When you're serving black punch with flies in it, a decorative crystal bowl is not required!

HAUNTED DRINKING CHOCOLATE

Rich and creamy with a haunting nip of cayenne and a hint of cinnamon, this hot chocolate gets its name from the mournful ghost who sits on the surface.

5 cups whole milk
1 cup half-and-half
⅓ cup Dutch process cocoa
⅓ cup sugar
¼ teaspoon ground cinnamon

⅛ teaspoon cayenne pepper
½ teaspoon vanilla extract
   marshmallow cream or whipped
    topping
8 chocolate chips

1. Bring the milk and half-and-half to a simmer in a medium saucepan over medium heat.

2. Mix the cocoa, sugar, cinnamon, and cayenne in a small bowl. Stir a few tablespoons of hot milk into the sugar until a thick, smooth paste is formed. Whisk this paste back into the pan of hot milk and add the vanilla. Taste and add more sugar if you prefer it a little sweeter.

3. Ladle the hot chocolate into 4 mugs and use a spoon to dollop out a large marshmallow cream or whipped topping ghost, using the back of the spoon to make a curl or twist on top of the head. Press on 2 chocolate chips for eyes. Serve immediately, before the ghosts melt and disappear into the hot depths.

SPIDERWEB PUMPKIN CHEESECAKE

Brown sugar adds mellow flavor to a rich pumpkin cheesecake, made worthy of a Halloween dinner party with a chocolate glaze and a spiderweb topping. (Make a plain chocolate glaze — no spiderweb — and this one will take you straight on to Thanksgiving!)

CRUST
- 16 graham crackers
- ¼ cup (½ stick) butter, melted
- 2 tablespoons sugar
- 1 teaspoon ground cinnamon

FILLING
- 2 (8-ounce) packages cream cheese, at room temperature
- ½ cup granulated sugar
- ½ cup firmly packed brown sugar
- 1 cup canned pumpkin purée (not pumpkin pie filling)
- 4 eggs
- 1 tablespoon pumpkin pie spice (page 87)
- 1 teaspoon vanilla extract

TOPPING
- 1 (6-ounce) package semisweet chocolate chips (1 cup)
- ¼ cup heavy cream
- ¼ cup sour cream

1. Preheat the oven to 325°F.

2. Crush the graham crackers in a food processor or put them in a heavy ziplock bag and beat and roll them with a rolling pin. Combine the crumbs, butter, sugar, and cinnamon. Press the mixture firmly into a 10-inch springform pan. Using the bottom of a glass, continue to press the crumbs into a compact crust.

3. Beat the cream cheese, granulated sugar, brown sugar, pumpkin, eggs, pumpkin pie spice, and vanilla until creamy and smooth. Pour the cream cheese mixture into the prepared crust and bake for 55 to 60 minutes, until firm in the center and not jiggly. Cool for at least 60 minutes in the pan on a rack. Leave the cheesecake in the pan and chill in the refrigerator for at least 6 hours, or overnight.

continued from previous page

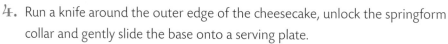

4. Run a knife around the outer edge of the cheesecake, unlock the springform collar and gently slide the base onto a serving plate.

5. Put the chocolate chips and the cream in a microwave-safe bowl, and melt in the microwave: Heat on high for 60 seconds, and then stir well. If it's not quite smooth, continue to heat in two or three 10-second bursts, stirring well after each burst. (Alternatively, you can melt the chocolate, stirring frequently, in a double boiler, over just-simmering water. Avoid overheating, which can cause chocolate to seize up into a stiff mass.) Pour the chocolate glaze over the chilled cheesecake, spreading just to the edges with a knife, but not going over the sides if you can avoid it.

6. Spoon the sour cream into a small ziplock bag and use a toothpick to poke a hole in one corner. Starting at the center of the cheesecake and working outward, drizzle a tight spiral of white across the top of the chocolate glaze.

7. Using a toothpick or the tip of a knife, gently pull through the sour cream and chocolate from the center to the outer edge. Continue to pull lines of sour cream, about 1 inch apart, wiping the toothpick between each pull. (See additional Spiderweb Decorating tips on page 58.)

8. Chill the spiderweb-topped cheesecake for about 15 minutes to set the glaze, but leave the cheesecake at room temperature at least 20 minutes before serving to mellow the flavor.

HALLOWEEN SUPPER

It's 6pm and the kids are hopping to get their costumes on and hit the pavements on their merry rounds. But no conscientious parent sends a child out to collect candy without a bellyful of supper first. Even though children recognize that this is ridiculous — all they want is to eat candy — parents have it imprinted genetically somewhere. So, although when I was a kid, I swore that one day I'd let my kids go out trick-or-treating without eating first and without a coat on to ruin their lovely costumes . . . you can guess what happens at our house.

You can alleviate some of the indignity of eating supper first by serving a highly Halloweeny meal, incorporating something ghostlike or something with a bit of pumpkin in it. The recipes here are for Halloween foods so tasty and child-friendly that your kids just might eat that much less candy.

ORANGE RICE WITH BACON (PUMPKIN RISOTTO)

While I could call this Pumpkin Risotto and serve it at a fancy dinner party, my children call it Orange Rice with Bacon and demand it for supper throughout the fall. It's a hearty and satisfying family meal when served with a green salad. If you're cutting up a large enough jack-o'-lantern, you can make it with the scraps of pumpkin flesh you trim off the lid and face pieces. The recipe calls for real chicken stock; if you have it, use it, but generally I use a stock cube in 3 cups of boiling water instead.

5 slices bacon, diced
3 cups chicken stock
3 tablespoons extra-virgin olive oil
1 medium yellow onion, chopped
2 garlic cloves, minced
1 pound pumpkin or butternut squash, diced into ½-inch cubes (about 4 cups)

scant 1 cup risotto rice, such as Arborio or Carnaroli
½ cup dry white wine
2 tablespoons butter
¼ cup shredded Parmesan cheese
salt and pepper

1. Fry the bacon in a large nonstick skillet until crisp. Drain on paper towels and set aside. Discard the fat in the skillet.

2. Bring the stock to a simmer in a small saucepan.

3. Heat the olive oil over medium heat in the same large skillet. Add the onion, garlic, and pumpkin cubes, and sauté for 5 to 6 minutes, until the onions are just translucent. Add the rice and cook, stirring, for 1 minute. Stir in the wine and simmer until it is nearly evaporated and the rice looks almost dry.

4. Add one ½-cup ladleful of the stock to the rice mixture and cook, stirring frequently until the liquid has been absorbed. Continue to add the broth in ½-cup increments, stirring frequently between additions, until the rice is just tender and creamy, about 15 minutes. Stir in the butter, Parmesan, and reserved bacon. Taste and add salt and pepper as needed. Serve immediately.

PUMPKIN SOUP WITH CHEESE CROUTONS

The problem with most pumpkin soups comes when people try to play up the natural sweetness of the squash. Leave the sweetness alone! The trick is to play up the savory aspects, best accomplished with a nice hit of garlic and sage, a bit of cayenne, and, best of all, a couple of big cheesy croutons floating on top. This is soup that truly does make a meal. If you think that your pumpkin's flesh may be watery, use butternut squash instead.

2 tablespoons extra-virgin olive oil
1 medium yellow onion, chopped
1 celery stalk, chopped
4 garlic cloves, minced
1 pound pumpkin or butternut
   squash, cubed (about 4 cups)
1 medium potato, peeled and diced
1 teaspoon dried sage
1 teaspoon salt
¼ teaspoon cayenne pepper
8 cups chicken stock

CROUTONS

12 slices French or
   Italian bread
   extra-virgin olive oil
1 garlic clove, peeled
   Parmesan, Gouda,
   cheddar, or any
   cheese you like,
   grated

1. Heat the olive oil in a large soup pot over medium heat. Add the onion, celery, and garlic, and sauté until lightly browned and softened. Add the pumpkin, potato, sage, salt, cayenne, and stock. Bring to a boil, lower the heat, and simmer for 30 minutes.

2. When the pumpkin and potato are tender, purée the soup with an immersion blender (or, carefully, in a blender). Taste and adjust the seasonings, adding more salt or cayenne as desired. Keep hot.

3. Toast the bread under the broiler until crisp and golden and then brush with olive oil. Rub the garlic clove lightly over one side (the crisp surface will grate off a light coating of garlic onto the bread). Sprinkle thickly with cheese and run back under the broiler for 1 or 2 minutes, until the cheese is melted.

4. Spoon the soup into bowls and float 2 croutons on each serving.

CANDY CORN PIZZA

Not made with candy corn — which is useful for decorating but may just be the sweetest candy in the world — but made to look *like* candy corn, which is a much tastier proposition. When you cut the hot pizza into triangles, the melted orange and white cheeses produce slices that look like big pieces of candy corn. You can use either a prebaked pizza crust, such as Boboli, or the ready-made pizza dough that can usually be found in the refrigerator section of the grocery store. You can also use either a jar of pizza sauce or a 6-ounce can of tomato sauce with basil, which is lighter tasting and doesn't have added sugar. Pizza is so forgiving — whatever you use, it will be good.

1 large pizza crust (or 1 pound pizza dough)

1 cup pizza sauce

8 ounces mozzarella, shredded (2 cups)

4 ounces orange cheddar cheese, shredded (1 cup)

1. Preheat the oven to 450°F. Put the pizza crust (or spread the pizza dough into a round) on a baking sheet sprinkled with cornmeal.

2. Smooth the sauce over the crust. Scatter the mozzarella in a thick circle in the very center of the pizza. Scatter the cheddar around the remaining space, leaving a visible rim of sauce and crust. (Keep the two cheeses as separate as possible so they melt into distinct rings of color for the best effect.)

3. Bake for 10 to 15 minutes if using a prebaked crust, or 20 minutes if using pizza dough. Cut into candy-corn triangles (which will show a white mozzarella tip, then an orange cheese middle and a line of red sauce and white crust), and serve immediately.

UNBLINKING EYE HALLOWEEN MEATLOAF

There are Halloween meatloaves made to look like body parts, but that goes over my personal squeamishness line. But I understand that an extra effort is needed for Halloween night and this one fills the bill: a row of peeled hard-boiled eggs inside makes each slice look like a monster eye on the dinner plate.

1 cup bread crumbs
½ cup milk
1 egg, lightly beaten
1 medium yellow onion, finely minced
1 medium carrot, shredded
1½ teaspoons salt
½ teaspoon black pepper

1 tablespoon Worcestershire sauce
1 tablespoon prepared horseradish
½ cup ketchup plus extra for glazing the loaf
1¼ pounds ground beef (or a meatloaf mixture of ground beef and pork)
4 hard-boiled eggs

1. Preheat the oven to 375°F. Lightly grease a 9- by 5-inch loaf pan.
2. Place the bread crumbs in a large bowl and pour in the milk and egg. Mix to combine; let the mixture stand for 10 minutes. The bread crumbs will absorb the liquid.
3. Add the onion, carrot, salt, pepper, Worcestershire, horseradish, and ketchup to the bread crumbs. Stir to combine.
4. Add the meat and incorporate all the ingredients well — hands are ideal for this. Layer half of the meat mixture in the bottom of the prepared pan.
5. Peel the hard-boiled eggs and lay them, end to end, down the middle of the pan on top of the meat layer. Pile the remaining meat mixture on top, smooth the surface, dollop with extra ketchup if desired, and bake for 45 minutes, until browned and cooked through; the internal temperature should be 160°F. Slice and serve immediately.

COLCANNON

Ireland invented Halloween, and while their more restrained traditions bear little resemblance to the excesses of the modern American holiday (when I was getting pillowcases full of candy as a child, my Dublin-born husband was innocently collecting apples and nuts from his neighbors), the Irish still take them very seriously. It's a rare home that doesn't serve Colcannon at least once around the end of October. Perhaps the best thing about real Irish Colcannon is the lake of melted butter traditionally added to the top of the mound. Tradition also dictates that a toy ring wrapped in foil or wax paper be buried within the potatoes; whoever forks up that bite is due to be married in the coming year.

1 pound curly kale, leaves stripped from tough stems	½ cup (1 stick) butter
2½ pounds potatoes	4 scallions, chopped
1½ cups whole milk	pinch of ground nutmeg
	salt and pepper

1. Bring a large pot of salted water to a boil, add the kale leaves, and cook for about 15 minutes, until tender but not mushy. Drain well and set aside to cool while you peel the potatoes.

2. Peel and quarter the potatoes and put them in a large saucepan. Cover with water and add a few teaspoons of salt. Bring to a boil and simmer until tender but not falling apart, about 20 minutes depending on the size of your potatoes.

3. While the potatoes are cooking, thinly slice the kale, discarding any tough stem pieces you may encounter.

4. Heat the milk in a small saucepan with 4 tablespoons of the butter and the scallions. Mash the potatoes with a masher or whip them with an electric mixer (never a food processor!); stir in the hot milk. Add the kale and nutmeg, and season to taste with salt and pepper. Serve in a large mound with the remaining 4 tablespoons of butter melted in a crater on top.

GHOSTLY MASHED POTATOES

Mashed potatoes enriched with butter and cheese and shaped into goofy ghosts are adorably cute and very, very good. They're an excellent accompaniment to any main dish throughout the month of October. The cheddar is optional but it helps the little ghosties to brown nicely in the oven.

- 8 medium potatoes (I like Yukon Gold)
- ½–¾ cup milk
- 4 tablespoons butter
- 2 ounces cheddar cheese, grated (about ½ cup), optional
- salt and pepper
- black sesame seeds, caraway seeds, or whole cumin seeds

1. Peel and quarter the potatoes and put them in a large saucepan. Cover with water and add a few teaspoons of salt. Bring to a boil and simmer until tender but not falling apart, about 20 minutes depending on the size of your potatoes.
2. Preheat the oven to 400°F. Lightly grease a baking sheet.
3. Drain the potatoes. Heat the milk and butter in a small saucepan or in the microwave. Mash the potatoes with a masher or whip them with an electric mixer (never use a food processor, which makes them gluey). Add ½ cup of the milk and butter and beat until smooth. If they seem stiff, add the remaining milk. Stir in the cheese, if desired, and season the potatoes to taste with salt and pepper.
4. Spoon the potatoes into a large ziplock bag (or a pastry bag fitted with a large plain tip), and cut an opening about ½ inch wide off one bottom corner. Pipe little conical ghosts about 4 inches tall onto the prepared baking sheet, pushing down the bag as you pipe to make a thicker base, then tapering upward to a narrow head. Push a couple of seeds into the head for eyes.
5. Bake the ghosts for about 15 minutes, until they are just browning around the edges. Serve immediately.

HAUNTED SHEPHERD'S PIE

Shepherd's Pie is ideal for Halloween night because it's a one-dish meal that will still taste good reheated if anyone is hungry after all that trick-or-treating.

1 recipe Ghostly Mashed Potatoes (page 132)
1½ pounds ground beef
1 carrot, grated
1 medium yellow onion, diced
3 tablespoons butter
3 tablespoons all-purpose flour

1¾ cups beef stock or broth
3 tablespoons ketchup
2 tablespoons Worcestershire sauce
salt and pepper
1 (10-ounce) package frozen peas
¼ cup Parmesan cheese, optional

1. Preheat the oven to 375°F and lightly grease a 3-quart casserole dish. Start the potatoes cooking for your Ghostly Mashed Potatoes before you turn to the beef.

2. Brown the beef in a large skillet over medium-high heat until no pink remains. Drain off any rendered fat. Push the meat to one side and sauté the carrot and onion for 4 to 5 minutes, until the onion is just turning translucent.

3. Push the onions and carrots to one side and melt the butter. Whisk the flour into the butter and then stir everything together. Add the stock, ketchup, and Worcestershire and cook for 5 minutes, until thickened. Season to taste with salt and pepper, and then stir in the peas.

4. Spoon the meat mixture into the prepared casserole dish. Smooth half the mashed potatoes from the ghost recipe over the surface and then pipe the remaining potatoes as ghosts on top, using the method described on page 132; add their sesame or caraway seed eyes. If desired, sprinkle the Parmesan cheese over and around the ghosts.

5. Bake for 20 to 25 minutes, until the sauce is bubbling and the ghosts are browned. Serve immediately.

Pumpkin-White Chocolate Bread

If you omit the white chocolate, this is a fragrant, flavorful, not-too-sweet pumpkin bread that's ideal for a Halloween breakfast or lunch, perhaps with a slather of cream cheese sandwiched between two thin slices. When you add the chips, it becomes a decadently delicious treat. This is my favorite, go-to quick bread for bake sales and brunches. The basic recipe works so well that you can vary it by adding raisins, dried cranberries, or nuts (pecans and walnuts are especially good), and it will always come out well.

1½ cups all-purpose flour
½ cup whole-wheat flour
1 cup sugar, plus more for sprinkling on top
2 teaspoons baking powder
1 teaspoon baking soda
½ teaspoon salt
1 teaspoon ground cinnamon
1 teaspoon ground ginger

½ teaspoon ground nutmeg
¼ teaspoon ground cloves
1 cup canned pumpkin purée (not pumpkin pie filling)
½ cup milk
2 eggs, beaten
4 tablespoons butter, melted
1 cup white chocolate chips

1. Preheat the oven to 350°F. Grease a 9- by 5-inch loaf pan.
2. Combine the all-purpose flour, whole-wheat flour, sugar, baking powder, baking soda, salt, cinnamon, ginger, nutmeg, and cloves in a large bowl.
3. Beat together the pumpkin, milk, eggs, and melted butter in a medium bowl. Fold into the flour mixture and stir just until blended. Add the white chocolate chips, and stir again, briefly, to combine. The batter should be lumpy.
4. Scrape the batter into the prepared loaf pan and sprinkle the surface generously with sugar. Bake for 65 minutes, or until a toothpick inserted in the center comes out with a few crumbs clinging. Cool in the pan for 10 minutes, and then turn out onto a wire rack to cool completely.

SCARY PARTY FOOD

You can make some party food scary simply by giving it a creepy name. For instance, roasted chicken wings are much more fun to eat on Halloween if a card placed near the serving dish identifies them as "Bat Wings," and a "Sandwich Graveyard" makes a platter of sandwiches much more Halloween-appropriate.

Other food actually looks kind of creepy, innocent as it is. While Worm Pie or Cup of Worms might take you into sugar overload, they are just gummy worms, set in Jell-O or buried in chocolate pudding and cookie crumbs. If you still enjoy eating gummy worms — I find I can live without them quite nicely as the years go by, but my kids feel differently — you probably won't find these dishes off-putting in the slightest.

All bets are off, however, when it comes to the scary foodstuffs that people feel, rather than eat. For a kids' party, I trot out the goopiest, yuckiest stuff I can think of to represent things like witch's guts (canned spinach) and intestines (soft manicotti stuffed with sour cream). And some items, such as dried apricots or torn flour tortillas, feel quite harmless in and of themselves, but when you hide them in a paper bag and call them mangled ears and flayed skin . . . well, the possibilities are endless.

FEELING SCARY

Handing around scary, goopy stuff in semidarkness is a perennial crowd-pleaser. It's not great for the littlest kids, who might get scared, and it's not great for teenagers, who might get bored (or at least say they are), but for that 'tween group of 8- to 12-year-olds, it's the stuff of which great Halloween parties are made. You can pass plastic bags around a circle, with appropriate intonations about what each contains, and let each child reach inside. Or, perhaps with a nod to better mess control, you can have bags, buckets, and bowls of stuff, and allow each child to come forward and feel them, which may be better for a small group. You can also set up stations of items on tables in a darkened room, with the bowls or plastic bags set down inside larger paper bags that are labeled with the contents, then invite the children to walk around and reach inside. Here are some fun and frightening things to feel:

INTESTINES Cooked manicotti or cannelloni noodles stuffed with sour cream

TONGUE A canned pear half, drained

BRAINS Cooked spaghetti, drained and immediately put into a rounded glass or metal bowl and chilled. (Once cold, it will hold its rounded shape when removed.)

EYEBALLS Peeled grapes or little marinated onions

FINGERS Drained can of Vienna sausages

FLAYED SKIN A few ripped pieces of soft flour tortilla

TOES Large and small dill pickles cut into appropriately sized pieces

DRAGON GUTS Green Jell-O made with 1 cup boiling water only, chilled, and cut into chunks

TUMORS A drained can of beets

EARS Pieces of dried apple or apricot

WITCH GUTS The contents of a can of spinach

BLOOD A box of red Jell-O mixed with ¾ cup boiling water; stir to dissolve and then serve it up warm (microwave the dish for a few seconds if your blood has cooled before party time)

Party Sandwich Graveyard

Among all the sweets, cakes, cookies, and candies, it's nice to have *some* form of savory food at a Halloween party; sandwiches are easy to make and kids will almost always eat them. For an appropriately eerie effect, cut the crusts off sandwich bread with a serrated knife, cutting down through 3 to 4 slices at a time (piling them any deeper can crush the bread). Then cut each slice in half and trim a slightly curved edge around the top to make bread tombstones. Fill with any of the toppings below and make a little graveyard of sandwiches on a platter lined with leaves of curly purple kale to serve as ground cover in your graveyard.

TUNA WITH OLIVE EYES 2 (6-ounce) cans tuna, drained and mixed with ¼ cup mayonnaise, ½ cup sliced pimento-stuffed green olives, and a dash of Tabasco

PIMENTO CHEESE WITH BLOODY SHREDS 2 cups grated sharp cheddar mixed with ½ cup mayonnaise, 1 (4-ounce) jar roasted red peppers (drained and chopped), 2 teaspoons Dijon mustard, 2 teaspoons Worcestershire sauce

PEANUT BUTTER AND STRAWBERRY JAM Crunchy peanut butter covered with just enough strawberry jam to ooze out the edges

CUCUMBER AND CREAM CHEESE 1 (8-ounce) package cream cheese, at room temperature, combined with 2 tablespoons lemon juice, salt and pepper to taste, 3 finely chopped scallions, and 1 large cucumber, peeled, grated, and squeezed dry

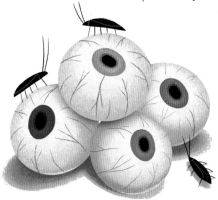

PUKING PUMPKINS

In the world of extreme pumpkin carving, jack-o'-lanterns with a wide-open mouth that appear to be barfing were a phenomenon a few years ago. Some were hurling their literal guts out, with a trail of pumpkins seeds and innards emanating from their mouths. Puking pumpkins are questionable in taste, but they are very funny on your Halloween party table. As a table decoration, carve a small pumpkin into a jack-o'-lantern with narrowed eyes and a gaping mouth. Prop it at the end of a serving tray, and tip it forward, either by putting a folded paper towel or newspaper up under its base, or by cutting a slice off one side of the base so it automatically sits with its face pointing toward the table. Then, beginning with the pumpkin's open mouth, spoon any of the following dips right into the front of the mouth and then in a trail down the length of your serving tray, placed in front of the pumpkin. For a neater, slightly less gross alternative, you can prop the tray right inside the pumpkin's mouth. It's goofy and kind of horrifyingly funny, but manages to be just *not* yucky enough for people to enjoy the food!

SALSA Use purchased salsa or make your own out of 1 (28-ounce) can whole tomatoes, drained and chopped, mixed with 1 diced white onion, the juice of 1 lime, ¼ cup diced pickled jalapenos, and salt to taste.

GUACAMOLE The purchased kind isn't nearly as good as homemade, which you can make by mashing the flesh of 3 or 4 perfectly ripe avocados with 1 finely minced onion and ⅓ cup fresh lime juice. Add chopped fresh cilantro and salt to taste.

SPINACH DIP Use purchased or follow the directions on the back of a package of Knorr Vegetable Soup Mix: you'll need 1 package soup mix, sour cream, mayo, thawed and drained frozen spinach, scallions, and water chestnuts.

For all three of these dips, surround the puking pumpkin's platter with tortilla chips — blue corn may look even creepier, in context, but the puking pumpkin itself is such a scene stealer that there's no need to go overboard with accompaniments.

BAT WINGS

As long as you call them bat wings, kids don't care what kind of sauce is actually on the chicken and grown-ups will be glad to see some real food. Preparing 5 pounds of pretrimmed wings for a party is actually pretty easy if you line a large rimmed baking sheet with foil (easy cleanup), lay out the wings, and sprinkle with salt and pepper. Roast in a 375°F oven for 35 to 40 minutes, until crisp and browned. Lift the wings out of the grease remaining on the foil (both of which you'll be discarding), and drop the wings into a large glass bowl in which you've already poured one of the sauces below. Toss and serve!

BUFFALO BATS Melt 1 stick of butter and stir in ¾ cup of mild hot sauce, such as Durkee's or Frank's.

SWEET AND SOUR BATS In a small saucepan, bring 1 (8-ounce) jar apricot preserves to a boil with ⅓ cup orange juice, ¼ cup red wine vinegar, and 2 tablespoons prepared horseradish. Cook 2 to 3 minutes to melt the preserves and thicken slightly.

MANCHURIAN BATS In a small saucepan, bring 1½ cups ketchup, 3 cloves minced garlic, and ½ teaspoon cayenne (or more to taste) to a boil. Cook for 2 to 3 minutes to mellow the garlic.

TERIYAKI BATS In a small saucepan, bring 1 cup low-sodium soy sauce, 1 cup ketchup, 2 tablespoons cider vinegar, and 2 tablespoons brown sugar to a boil. Cook for 5 minutes, until slightly thickened.

CUP OF WORMS

This creepy dessert couldn't be simpler: chocolate pudding, cookie crumbs, and gummy worms. But kids love it so much more than they could ever love that génoise sponge with Italian meringue and candied violets that took you two days to make! Go figure.

       2 (3.5-ounce) boxes instant
             chocolate pudding mix
       4 cups milk
      24 chocolate wafers or 12 chocolate
             sandwich cookies, such as
             Oreos
          gummy worms
          unsweetened cocoa powder

1. Prepare the chocolate pudding with the milk, according to the package directions.
2. Place the cookies in a heavy ziplock bag and crush by beating and rolling them with a rolling pin or a wine bottle.
3. Put the gummy worms on a plate and sprinkle lightly with a few teaspoons of cocoa, rolling them to coat.
4. Put 2 to 3 tablespoons of pudding in the bottom of each of 8 clear plastic cups or glass custard cups. Drop 1 gummy worm into each cup. Top with the remaining pudding, then top each with the crumbs. Place 3 worms on top of each cup. Chill until ready to serve.

JIGGLY EYEBALLS

You can use frozen blueberries as the pupils in these jiggly Jell-O eyes, or try raisins, dried cherries, or dried cranberries if you prefer, but be sure to use something edible since children, unaccountably, actually seem to enjoy eating the eyeballs! Don't follow the standard package directions when making the Jell-O. Here, you're using less than half the amount of water called for on the box in order to make eyeballs that hold their shape. You will need an ice-cube tray with rounded bottoms to create a credible eye shape.

    2 **(3-ounce) boxes lemon Jell-O**
1¼ **cups boiling water**
 24 **blueberries or raisins**

1. Put the Jell-O in a medium bowl and cover with the boiling water. Stir with a spoon until the gelatin has dissolved.

2. Spoon a few teaspoons of the prepared Jell-O into each compartment of an ice-cube tray with a rounded bottom. The cubes should be only half-filled. Set in the freezer for about 15 minutes until set.

3. Drop a blueberry or raisin into each cube and cover with the remaining Jell-O. Chill in the refrigerator until firm. Pop out and line up on a serving plate or mound into a bowl, rounded side up.

BAG O' DIRT

These goofy party favors for the littlest goblins look deceptively plain on first inspection: a plastic ziplock bag full of dirt made out of cookie crumbs. You can just hear them thinking, "Gee, thanks a lot." But invite your little guests to squeeze the packages and start searching inside with a spoon — the crumbs hide a terrific grab-bag of goodies, from gummy worms and spider rings to candy pumpkins and ghostly Peeps. After they've mined for goodies, suggest that they take their dirt home to use as an ice cream topping.

24 chocolate sandwich cookies, such
    as Oreos (about half of an
    18-ounce package)
candy and little plastic toys such as
    spider rings

1. Crush the cookies to fine crumbs in a food processor or place them in a large ziplock bag and crush them with a rolling pin or wine bottle. Divide the crumbs among 8 ziplock sandwich bags.
2. Divide your loot among the bags, pushing the candy and toys down into the crumbs. Seal the bags and shake and turn them to hide all the goodies inside.

Worm Pie

Kids can never have enough gummy worms, but this worm pie might come as close as anything to doing the trick. Multicolored worms seem to turn and spin in a quivering mound of yellow Jell-O. It's not really for eating, but don't be surprised if they do. Make it in a clear glass pie plate so you can see the worms within; otherwise you will have to unmold the pie.

> **gummy worms**
> 1 **(3-ounce) package yellow or orange Jell-O**
> 1 **cup boiling water**
> ½ **cup cold water**

1. Grease a 9-inch glass pie plate with vegetable oil and lay a thick crop of gummy worms across the bottom.
2. Pour the gelatin into a medium bowl and add the boiling water, stirring until the gelatin has dissolved. Add the cold water to the Jell-O and allow to cool almost to room temperature before pouring it over the worms; refrigerate. After about 1 hour, if any of the worms are floating on top, use your finger to push them down into the thickening Jell-O.
3. Serve in the glass dish or, if you like, turn over and unmold onto a serving plate.

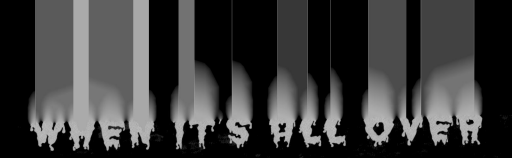

WHEN IT'S ALL OVER

As a child, I often woke up on November 1 with a sense of anticlimax. After the thrills and chills of the night before, including the all-important candy swap with my siblings on the living room floor — "I'll trade you 10 Sweet Tarts for 1 miniature Snickers" — it felt as if my stash of candy had already lost some of its magic in the light of day.

But candy is candy, so we gorged ourselves for several days (at least, as often as our parents would allow) until we were sated and sick on the stuff. After a week, our sacks sat unmolested in the kitchen pantry, alongside any leftovers from the candy we gave out at the door that year.

Still, it's a shame to throw away all that hard-earned candy, collected with such vigor and enthusiasm. As the years went by, I began to hear stray murmurs about ways to use up all that "unwanted" candy. And what do you know? Several of them are really fun and even delicious!

Take these revived goodies to bake sales, potlucks, or school birthday parties, and you'll hear nothing but raves. However, be sure to use your very best leftovers — these baked goods are crying out for chocolates, caramel, and peanuts. Don't chop up hard candies, Peeps, gummy worms, or other novelties. In fact, fond as I am of all things Halloween, you might consider throwing those kinds of leftovers away after a few weeks. Don't for-

HALLOWEEN AFTER-CAKE

With the flavor of a rich, buttery pound cake and an appealingly dense crumb, this is a perfect "cutting" cake — ideal to have on hand for an afternoon pick-me-up or as a sweet treat to go into a school lunch. Tossing the chopped candy with flour helps prevent it from sinking to the bottom of the cake. For the best results, bring all the ingredients, eggs included, to room temperature before mixing the cake.

- 2 cups all-purpose flour
- 1 teaspoon baking powder
- ½ teaspoon salt
- 1 cup (2 sticks) butter, at room temperature
- 1 cup sugar

- 4 eggs
- 1 teaspoon vanilla extract
- ½–¾ cup coarsely chopped chocolate candies, tossed with 2 tablespoons flour

1. Preheat the oven to 350°F. Grease a 9- by 5-inch loaf pan and dust lightly with flour.
2. Combine the flour, baking powder, and salt in a small bowl and set aside.
3. Cream the butter and sugar in a large bowl with an electric mixer until fluffy, about 5 minutes. One at a time, beat in the eggs, incorporating each egg well, and then add the vanilla. With the mixer on low, beat in the flour mixture. Stir in the chopped candy and scrape the batter into the prepared pan.
4. Bake for 60 minutes, until golden brown, and a cake tester or toothpick inserted in the center comes out clean. Cool in the pan for 20 minutes, and then turn the cake out and place it right side up on a rack to cool completely.

HALLOWEEN AFTER-COOKIES

The buttery batter for these cookies is studded with chewy oatmeal and nuggets of your favorite candy bars. If you have a unifying theme to your candy stash — be it Butterfingers or Snickers, Milky Ways, Almond Joys, or Hershey's Miniatures — try making these cookies with all one type of candy bar.

1 cup (2 sticks) butter, at room temperature	1 teaspoon baking powder
1½ cups firmly packed brown sugar	½ teaspoon baking soda
¼ cup granulated sugar	½ teaspoon salt
2 eggs	3½ cups rolled oats
2 teaspoons vanilla extract	1 cup coarsely chopped chocolate candies
1¾ cups all-purpose flour	

1. Preheat the oven to 350°F. Cream the butter, brown sugar, and granulated sugar with an electric mixer until fluffy, 3 to 4 minutes. Beat in the eggs and vanilla. Add the flour, baking powder, baking soda, and salt; stir until combined. Fold in the oats and chopped candy.

2. Spoon large dollops of dough — about 3 tablespoons per cookie — onto ungreased baking sheets, leaving 2 to 3 inches between cookies. Flatten slightly with the bottom of a glass (dip the base in a bit of sugar if the glass sticks to the dough).

3. Bake for 12 to 15 minutes, until just set and golden but not brown. Transfer to a rack to cool.

HALLOWEEN AFTER-CUPCAKES

Under their innocent exteriors, these post-Halloween cupcakes hide a secret candy center that surprises and delights kids. Yellow cake with a milk chocolate frosting highlights the flavor inside, but you can use any cake or frosting combination that you like. These are ideal for a school bake sale or a kid's birthday party.

1 recipe yellow cupcakes, from
   Wormy Cupcakes (page 94)
18 pieces miniature chocolate candy,
   unwrapped

1 recipe milk chocolate frosting
   (page 94)

1. Preheat the oven to 350°F. Line 18 cups in two 12-cup muffin tins with paper liners.

2. Prepare the cupcake batter according to directions. Fill each liner one-third full and drop a candy on top. Add more batter to fill each tin two-thirds or just slightly less full of batter. Don't overfill or the cupcakes will bulge out the top, making them more difficult to frost and upsetting the proper cake-to-candy ratio!

3. Bake for 12 to 15 minutes, until a tester or toothpick inserted in the center comes out clean. Cool cupcakes completely and then frost with milk chocolate frosting. (If you have a real glut of leftover candy, unwrap another 18 pieces and place one on top of each cupcake.)

INDEX

Other Storey Titles You Will Enjoy

Cookie Craft, by Valerie Peterson & Janice Fryer.
Clear instruction, practical methods and all the tips and tricks
for beautifully decorated special occasion cookies.
168 pages. Hardcover. ISBN 978-1-58017-694-1.

The Good-to-Go Cookbook, by Kathleen Cannata Hanna.
Hundreds of recipes to feed busy families, from weeknight dinners that
take to 15 minutes to prepare to relaxed suppers for the weekend.
336 pages. Paper. ISBN 978-1-60342-076-1.

The Perfect Pumpkin, by Gail Damerow.
Detailed instructions on how to grow and harvest more than
95 varieties, plus fun craft ideas and great recipes.
224 pages. Paper. ISBN 978-0-88266-993-9.

Pumpkin, by DeeDee Stovel.
A wide-ranging collection of recipes, from soups to desserts
and everything in between that use this nutritious orange super food.
224 pages. Paper. ISBN 978-1-58017-594-4.

Scarecrows, by Felder Rushing.
Inspiring color photos of scarecrow art from around the world,
matched with 20 projects, from the traditional to the surprising.
112 pages. Paper. ISBN 978-1-58017067-3.

These and other books from Storey Publishing are available
wherever quality books are sold or by calling 1-800-441-5700.
Visit us at *www.storey.com*.